SOCCER
MODERN TACTICS

ITALY'S TOP COACHES ANALYZE GAME FORMATIONS
THROUGH 180 SITUATIONS

ALESSANDRO ZAULI

Translation by
Paola Milan

**Library of Congress
Cataloging - in - Publication Data**

by Alessandro Zauli
   SOCCER - MODERN TACTICS

ISBN No. 1-59164-025-3
Lib. of Congress Catalog No. 2002107549
© 2002

Layout and Art Direction
Bryan R. Beaver

Reedswain Publishing
88 Wells Road
Spring City, PA 19475
800.331.5191
www.reedswain.com
info@reedswain.com

CONTENTS

Chapter 3. Principles of the offensive stage

Chapter 4. Offensive work for different formations

Chapter 5. The defensive stage with 3 players

Chapter 6. Offensive exercises for different formations

Chapter 7. Individual tactics for defense and attack

Chapter 8. Management of the formation in the junior team

PREFACE

How can we define this book? The coaches' perfect manual? The guide to winning every match? Not at all. This book should only inspire and function as a starting point for those who want to go deeper in their studies and - perhaps - one day write a better book.

Here I tried to analyze the issues related to the zone formations. I did not only propose some training exercises, I also wanted to offer the tools to solve the several issues that arise during a match.

If this book fosters discussions, objections and arguments, then I'll have reached my goal. I'm proud to present a text where there are 10 interviews with high level professional coaches, in which we have the chance to look at the tactical formations even more deeply.

This is a book written by a coach like any other, who's been on the field for 16 years and who's hoping that all his readers have a great love for clean soccer. Every coach, from Serie A to the Junior Team, should be professional and do his best for his players.

I hope and wish that this book will help you to improve your knowledge of game formations.

Alessandro Zauli

LEGEND FOR DIAGRAMS

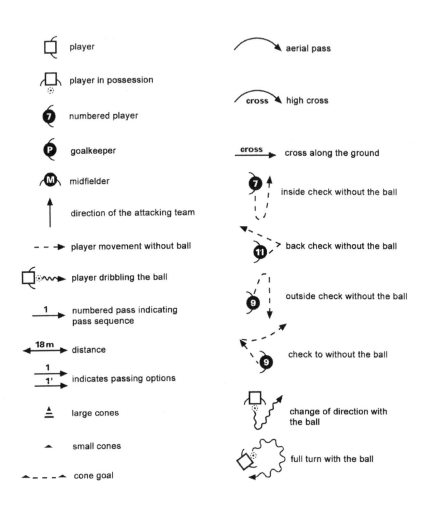

player

player in possession

numbered player

goalkeeper

midfielder

direction of the attacking team

player movement without ball

player dribbling the ball

numbered pass indicating pass sequence

distance

indicates passing options

large cones

small cones

cone goal

aerial pass

high cross

cross along the ground

inside check without the ball

back check without the ball

outside check without the ball

check to without the ball

change of direction with the ball

full turn with the ball

Before starting to analyze the methodology for training our teams in the best way, it is good to clarify what we will base our statements on:

▶ To determine the concept of closing down the opposing player in possession;
▶ To determine the stages for controlling the opposing player in possession;
▶ To determine the marking of the opponent or the marking of the opposition not in possession according to zone principles;
▶ To challenge the attacking player in possession;
▶ To challenge the attacking player in possession and other challenging players;
▶ To neutralize the opposition's slicing shots in deep;
▶ To neutralize the opposition's triangular-passing;
▶ To neutralize the opposition's overlapping;
▶ To neutralize the opposition's long shots;
▶ To neutralize penetrating passes to the opposition's forwards;
▶ To determine the behavior of the back line during back pass maneuvers;
▶ To determine the behavior of the back line when in situations of numerical inferiority or with players out of position;
▶ To determine quick game shifts;
▶ To determine marking against crosses.

Then we will also consider those situations where the midfield area is added to the defense. We will analyze the doubling-up of defenders and midfield players, together with the unfolding (this time with two positions) of the situations listed above. Finally we will add the attack and the layout of our team formation will be complete.
We would like to clarify that these exercises require the understanding of a few basic defensive principles, such as the conduct in defensive 1 v 1 and the concept of marking players without the ball (by zone or by man). Without this kind of knowledge it will be difficult for the players to

understand the position exercises or the team exercises that we propose
here.

1.1 Coming out and control of the opponent in possession

A basic principle of any defensive phase is the cover given by the
defender placed diagonally behind the first defender, ready to act in case
the attacker beats him.

Let's look at **diagram 1**: the coach points to a player (A/B/C/D) and
gives him the ball; in this case A is the player in possession. We see the
position using 2 to come out and pressure him, with 4 covering, and 3
and 6 aligned with him and getting closer to the ball - but not too close -
to avoid the risk of a possible switch of play.

The same happens with the ball on D.

This kind of defense is called one line cover. On the other hand, if we
wish to play with a double cover, 6 is placed diagonally towards 4, with 3
aligned with 4 **(diagram 2)**.

There is also a triple cover where 3 is aligned diagonally with 6 as well.
If the ball, instead, is controlled by B or C - in other words it is placed
centrally **(diagram 3)** - the defense is positioned as a pyramid, with 4
coming out on the player in possession and 2 and 6 distributed in a triangle for covering and 3 closing the field.

The exercise continues with players A,B,C or D passing the ball at the
sound of the coach's whistle. In this case the approach to the opposing
player - who will receive the ball - becomes quite important.

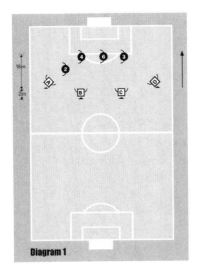

Diagram 1

Diagram 2

It is fundamental to move quickly towards the player receiving a long pass and then to stop just before he receives it.

In this way we close down the receiver, limiting him in space and time and restricting his passing options, especially deep penetrating passes, which is what a defense fears the most.

During the development of the next exercise the players pass the ball randomly between each other.

Then we add one or two passive players on the defensive line, who only move horizontally before each pass and need to be marked. We have to keep in mind that:

Good marking means:

- to be between the opponent and the goal;
- to see the player in possession and the player off the ball who needs to be marked;
- to tightly mark the opponent, if the player in possession does not see the goal or if the attacker is near the goal, or the player in possession sees the goal but cannot shoot;
- to mark more loosely if the player in possession sees the goal and can shoot or your player is very far from the ball.

These principles are true both for man-to-man-marking and zone-marking. The difference is that with man-to-man marking, the player will be followed anywhere on the field and there will be direct contact with him at all times. With the zone-marking, defenders mark the players only when they are in their zone, otherwise they are left to other teammates.

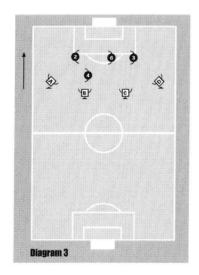

Diagram 3

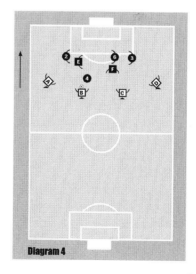

Diagram 4

This means a change in the points of reference. For zone marking these are ball-zone-man and for man marking these are ball-man.

See **diagram 4**: as the ball is with B, we see 6 guarding 4 and correctly marking F; on the other hand 2 is on the outer side of E and not between him and the goal, and this is why he has to change his position.

So with each pass it's important to verify that each defender is marking and covering in the right way.

To complete this first paragraph, we must analyze how many covering lines it is convenient to use in the many game situations.

In the preceding pages we saw that - when the ball is on the side of the field - the defensive diagonal can be laid out as 1, 2 or 3 covering lines. This choice changes depending on several variables such as:

▸   our defenders are not very capable or too slow in the defending 1v1 situations;

▸   we play against attackers who are very good or very fast in 1 v 1 situations and we tend to use a multiple covering line;

▸   we have players who are very fast and very good in the defending 1v1 situations and we can use a single covering line.

As in all situations, there are good and bad things. If we play with more than one covering line, our opponents will attack in depth, whereas if we use a single covering line, we will have to be certain of our defenders' skills, as we said earlier.

We see in **diagram 5** that as the ball is moving between A,B,C and D and it gets to the outside players, they can position themselves where they can either see the opponents' goal or not.

In the first case (diagram 5), since the player in possession cannot pass it on (he's turning his back), the back line is laid out as a covering line. In fact, in that moment A is not dangerous and there is no need to act differently.

Also the front men E and F will be marked closely because the player in possession cannot see the goal.

The situation represented in **diagram 6** is different. The player in possession is able to see the goal and the defense plays with a double covering line. A

Diagram 5

triple covering line would be too much and allow the opponents to get too deep.

1.2   Passing the marking duties from one defender to the next

According to the zone principles there is not a set marking pattern. An opponent is controlled by a defender depending on the area he is moving in. This is true for the players without the ball, but also for the player holding the ball. For instance let's take a look at **diagram 7**: A dribbles the ball and 2 closes him, then he dribbles the ball into the sector controlled by 4. At this point 4 calls out to 2 (who can't see him since he's turning his back) to leave the player in possession to him. 2 quickly returns to cover 4, who is now marking the player in possession. The exercise goes on with A "invading" the areas guarded by 6 and 3 who will pass the marking over to one another. In the same way the player in possession can always dribble back and forth. It is very important that the player in possession is marked at all times. Too often the player passes the marking to a teammate too soon, before the new defender is there. This creates a very dangerous temporary gap where the player in possession can play deep or slide into a free space. We have the opposite problem when 2 is out and when 2 is in. While the defender closes the player in possession, his teammate - who's about to receive the marking role - places himself in line with him (without covering him).

The player who is about to receive the marking role has to move close to the player in possession, but continues to cover his teammate, until it's

Diagram 6

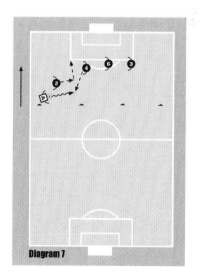

Diagram 7

5

time to quickly pass him on. In this position we apply the principle of 3 in and 1 out (on the runner).

To keep a short distance: in all the situations between the player who moves to mark the player in possession of the ball and the other 3, the distance does not have to be too great. If this happens, the passage of the marking becomes difficult because the new marker has to run too far to mark the player in possession who entered his zone and also the "old" marker has to run too far to cover. This would complicate the whole inter-change of positions.

Never in one line: it is always necessary to maintain the covering of the marking player (even when his back is turned the other way). A sudden turn from this player can be very dangerous for the defense in one line and without cover because - if the 1 v 1 succeeds - it will allow an easy access to the goal.

To advance up-field without losing the man-markings: when the ball is moved away from the goal, the team (especially the defenders) must move up-field the same distance as the player in possession of the ball. The player in possession cannot see the goal and so he cannot play the ball deep. However, if there are one or more attacking men on the defensive back line, we have to keep in mind the following: as we move up-field, if the attacking men don't get back, they will be offside; if they do get back, it is necessary to continue marking them, according to the principle that we must be able to always see the ball and the opponent. This is to keep the player in possession, who has changed direction suddenly, from finding deep unmarked teammates.

Later on we will add one and then two passive players without ball. With their presence we will force the defenders to relate with their marking duties. Another change comes from the visual attitude of the dribbler during the lead; when he is in the side area, he can lead looking at the goal, forcing the defense to a double cover; or - if he's not able to see the goal and the back line - he will place himself on one covering line.

1.3   Neutralizing deep penetrating runs

Penetrating runs behind the defense can be very dangerous if they are not faced carefully. In **diagram 8** we see 2 going out on A, who - after dribbling for a few yards - serves E who has just cut in behind 2 and in front of 4.

A cut is a movement that, by itself, allows you to receive the ball even before the defender, since the attacking player places his body between the defender and the ball.

Very important: to avoid this it's not enough to have the defender aligned with the attacker, but he has to delay him a bit (in other words he has to be a little ahead of him) to prevent him from receiving the ball.

The cutting-in is always the responsibility of the player who can see it. In this case it's surely within the field of 4 and not 2, who is turning his back.

In this exercise we can introduce two variables: the dribbler can delay the pass on purpose and in this case 4 cannot go with E endlessly. At some point 4 leaves him to get back to his place with the other three defenders.

When does this happen? It happens when E moves beyond the last defender (offside). Who calls out for E? It's the last defender (in this case 6) because he's the one who can see better and he is the last defender. It is obvious that this system depends on how many covering lines one wants to use. In case of one line it's the same player who is marking, since he knows all the other players are aligned with him. Then we move up-field attacking the dribbler, but we keep all the players covering to ensure that - since E is in passive offside - the referee does not allow the action to continue and the dribbler's breakthrough is faced in a thoughtful way.

It can also happen that the dribbler, instead of passing to E, who is making a cut, dribbles to the inside. If he does, we have to follow this one rule: if there is time, we pass the marking to one another, if not, we adopt a defending intersection.

In the first case 4 is able to let E take his place again in order to face the dribbler; in the second case 4 is not able to do it and continues to follow E, and 2 keeps closing the dribbler inside. Of course 4 will have to say it aloud to 2 (because his back is turned). The exercise has to be repeated with A holding the ball and cutting between 4 and 6 and 6 and 2; also with B or C holding the ball in midfield and various players making the cuts.

Diagram 8

7

1.4   Neutralizing triangular passing

These are movements with two players trying to beat the defender. They are called one-twos (from the number of passes) or triangles (from the geometric shape described by the ball trajectories). These movements get the ball behind the defender. If done at the right moment and with the right speed, they are very dangerous. In **diagram 9** A focuses on 2 - who is closing the player down - and then together with E tries to create a triangle behind him. In order not to be overcome by it, as soon as A gives the ball to E and cuts behind the defender, 2 turns towards the outside and moves quickly to intercept the ball; 4, 6 and 3 do the same and move away.

Very important: if 2 is approached by the dribbler, he should move back, cutting on player A, and since they basically have started at the same level (but with A set on a straight line and with 2 needing to turn around), the defender is not in a good position to move towards the ball anymore. As the defender moves in, he shouldn't stop because he could block the opponent. He has to act as a mobile defensive shield.

If 2 doesn't allow the dribbler to approach him, he can run back to the ball since he finds himself in a good position.

The attitude of 4 is also very important. On the pass from A to E, player 4 should move in if he has the chance to successfully challenge for the ball. If it's not possible, he has to move back to avoid being taken out of the play completely. Players have to be careful near the penalty area because - with the defenders going back - E could decide to hold the ball

Diagram 9

Diagram 10

and not to pass to A.

On the other hand he could kick the ball from the edge of the area or a bit further. This would be very dangerous because 4 would not have the time to tackle him. **Diagram 10** shows very clearly the triangle situation in midfield. The safety system is more sophisticated: B dribbles towards 4 and calls E for a triangle. Also, 2 and 6 move back, creating a "chain". In this case too 6 will have to calculate if he can delay E or not. The exercise with the ball on B and C has to be repeated with E on the right and the left side in order to involve all players in the many triangular passes.

1.5   Neutralizing overlapping

These are movements behind the dribbler trying to create a 2 v 1 situation in favor of the attackers. When near the ball the numerical superiority of the opponents is very dangerous and has to be "defused" very quickly. In **diagram 11** B passes over to A and cuts behind him, creating a lateral 2 v 1. 2 moves closer to A, but he avoids entering into his range and moves back to give 4 the time to get closer, thereby restoring numerical equality. When 4 is in place, ready to close the dribbler down, he tells 2 who should mark B.

Very important:

▶   2 must not allow the dribbler to get too close because, by passing the ball to B, he could easily settle it with a 2 v 1;

▶   as 2 moves back he should be able to see the dribbler and B overlapping;

▶   2 should play for time and apply the principle that when you are in numerical inferiority you should delay and wait for help. The dribbler should be immediately attacked with the appropriate marking only when he stretches out to foster a tackle or when B is offside. The exercise must be done on the right and on the left.

Diagram 11

1.6   Neutralizing shots and headers

To avoid getting caught by surprise by a shot coming from behind the defensive line, the marking must always be correct.

If the dribbler can see, the marking will be slow, otherwise it will be tight. This is to destroy the myth that the defense should always be on one line (it never is!) with fast central players. If the defenders are slow but good in marking, it's not a big problem. Of course if a slow defender and a fast attacker are on the ball at the same time, it's easy to concede a goal. It becomes fundamental to correctly mark the opposition's attackers at all times.

As the ball is shot, the players move back with a tactical cross-step run. They don't move back with a regular run (it would not be very fast and balanced), but with a run set on the side and being ready to change direction, pivoting on the back foot. After moving back, the engaged player will move towards the ball as the other players secure the marking.

If the players leave this position too soon, there could be some problems: our team could stretch out too much and allow the opponents - who pretend to make a long pass - to play short passes with our players positioned too far away. This would clearly make the defensive marking very difficult.

See **diagram 11b**; the 4 players pass the ball to each other and the defense slides to the right, left and midfield, without coming out on the dribbler or moving back and forth. The danger comes not when the ball moves horizontally, but when the dribbler attacks vertically or when the ball moves deep through a short pass or a long ball. Notice that when A or B have the ball, 2 and 3 move near the big cones on the side. Then we place two forwards (C and D) on the defensive line and, depending on the behavior of the player in possession (either they see the goal or not), the defenders slowly or tightly mark C and D who are not moving.

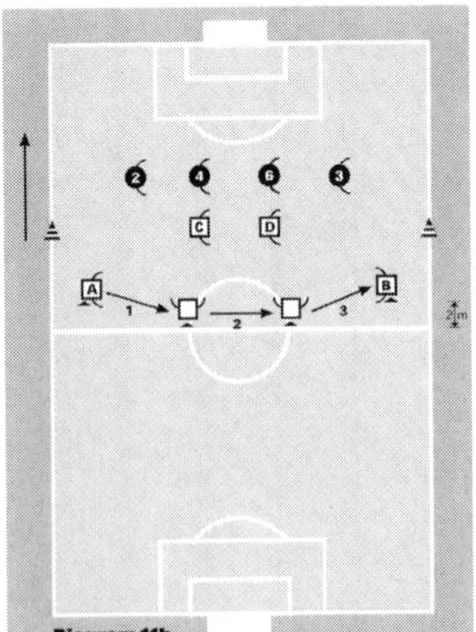

A new variable comes from the fact that the player in possession can shoot, as the two forwards move deep trying to get the ball. This exercise is very important to understand the marking of

Diagram 11b

the forwards so that you are not caught by surprise (too close) when the ball gets passed over.

If the forwards move deep too soon, it is necessary to go with them and then move back.

To successfully block the headers of attackers good in the air, we have to analyze the situation very carefully.

In fact there are some teams that, in order to beat the opponents' pressure, pass a high ball to one of the forwards who then sends it to another player cutting in behind the defensive line. A ball in the air can be easily sent deep with any part of the body.

After dribbling the ball, we see (**diagram 12**) one of the 4 players marking (high) the attacker C, who fakes a backward-upward pass to elude the marking. While 6 closes him down, E receives the ball and passes into space behind the defender. 2, 4 and 3 move tightly towards the ball to secure the cover. One variable comes from the presence of D and E who, during the air maneuver, move deep up field trying to win the ball. E places himself once on the right side and once on the left.

1.7 Neutralizing penetrating passes

The opposing attackers can also receive the ball at their feet rather than deep up field. In this case we have to prevent them from turning around because they could dribble towards the defensive line and help other players to cut in.

Diagram 13 shows us the case: as the 4 players pass the ball to one

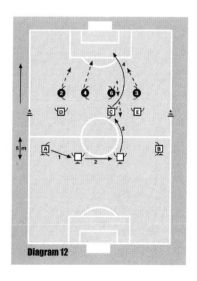

Diagram 12

Diagram 13

another, C fakes a run up field and instead receives the ball and tries to turn around. The defensive line has to prevent this. And if C is able to turn around, the defenders have to neutralize him.

Very important: the player (in this case 4) who is closing down C, has to approach him quickly while the ball is moving. Placing himself on one side he stops just before the attacker receives the ball. With his arm out he has to "feel" C and be sure that:

▸ the distance prevents the attacker from leaning on his body and turning around;

▸ the distance prevents the attacker from pivoting and beating him one on one.

The defender, facing the attacker's back, has to be patient and look for a tackle when the attacker is halfway through turning with the ball. In fact this is the time when he is less able to defend the ball using his body.

When 4 closes C down, the formation covers him to guarantee the necessary marking and the 4 players stay close to each other. It could happen that the player closing the attacker is too far from the other three. This creates problems when they have to exchange marking duties.

1.8   Conduct for back passes

A back pass by the opponents is a chance for our team to gain ground and move up-field. A lot depends on the length of the back pass. Normally when the back passes are short we don't move up-field because there is not time to maneuver, stop and position the players again. But when the back passes are long, we move up and stop just before the opponent receives the ball. The length of the pass gives us the time to move the team up.

On a back pass, the defense should move quickly forward while the ball is in motion. During this time the ball cannot be played and consequently it's not dangerous. Just before the opponent receives the ball, the defense should stop and take position.

After stopping, the defensive line places the players on one side (and not in front),"reads" the new position of the opponent in possession and acts accordingly.

Very important: as they move up-field, the defenders don't have to stop marking the opponents. The opposing attackers on the defensive line, in order to avoid the offside trap created by the line's progression, will also have to move towards midfield. During this movement the defender must keep his eyes on the opposing receiver and on the opponent in his zone (marking principle).

Let's look at **diagram 14**: the 4 players dribble the ball (with two for-wards on the defensive line) and the defense practices coming out on the player in possession and covering. Pay attention when C or B has the ball. Depending on whether they can see or not, the cover line will be one or two.

When the ball is moving, it is possible to pass back to:
▶   A (right behind the players in possession);
▶   A1 (10-12 yards in the other half of the field)
The two players can be in the middle of the field, on the right or on the left.
If A receives the ball, he plays it back with a short pass to one of the 4 players. If A1 receives the ball, we stop the game and start all over again. A variable comes from the introduction of two attackers on the defensive line who - in case of a long back pass during the progression of the posi-tion - don't have to get lost. We have one last variable when A or A1 - after receiving - plays a short ball or a long pass.
If the ball is passed back to A1, it's clear that the 4 dribblers and the two attackers have moved forward to avoid the offside trap.

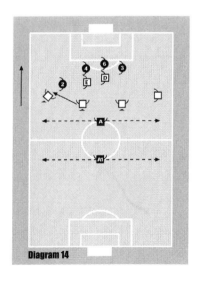

Diagram 14

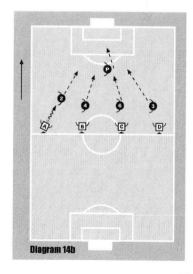

Diagram 14b

13

1.9   Position of the line

A basic principle says that if the player is in a good position, he has to come out and close the dribbler down. In other words, this happens when the players on the defensive line are close to each other and able to guarantee the cover.

When there is a lot of space behind the marker, the position is not good. In this case we have to move back, compact the position again and play closer to our goalkeeper. This is obvious, but logical: it's easier to mark in a small space than in a bigger one.

Diagram 14b shows us this situation: A moves towards the line that is wide and near midfield. The defensive line moves back and the players get closer to each other. At this point the first marker comes out on the dribbler and passes the marking to his teammates with each change of direction.

Then the exercise is repeated with the dribbler coming from a central position and finally from the other side. When the ball is central, the line moves back with all the players turned towards the inside of the field. The goalkeeper participates in this maneuver, starting from a "high" position and moving back with the line. Now we add two attackers to the defensive line. When the exercise is well understood, we add a few variables to make it more difficult: some cutting in opponents will create triangles or overlaps to get behind the line while the defenders move closer to one another. This forces the defense to face a tense situation. The defenders must compact very quickly and immediately solve a new problem.

1.10   When the defensive line is in a situation of numerical inferiority

Here it's still valid what we have said in the paragraph above. It doesn't make sense to mark the opposing player in possession if we are not in a good position. This includes when we are in a situation of numerical inferiority. In this case we have two chances:

▸   to delay as we move back and get closer, waiting for our player to be back in position;

▸   to delay as we move back and get closer without waiting for help from a teammate; this could happen when there is a very fast action of the opponents or when we lose possession of the ball in the goal area.

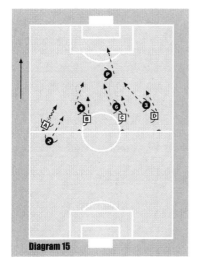

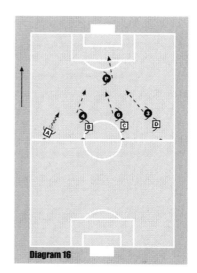

Diagram 15

Diagram 16

Diagram 15 shows us this situation: A is in possession of the ball and starts moving. Also 2, who is behind A, moves to get to his position. Meanwhile 4, 6 and 3 move back getting closer and the attackers B, C and D move forward. When 2 is back on the defensive line, it's time to come out on the player in possession and exchange the marking duties with the other 3 forwards. The exercise has to be repeated without 4, 6 and 2 (alternating) and with the ball moving from these positions.

Very important: the run of 2 to gain the ball must be on a diagonal line towards the inside of the field. This is the shortest way to the goal area and to the defenders. The choice of which defender will come out on the opposing attacker will depend on where 2 is placed. The fundamental thing is to have 4 players, it doesn't matter how they are laid out. In case there are no players coming to help, it's necessary to accept the numerical inferiority and take advantage of the opponents' mistakes.

There are two opponents' mistakes that we can use:

▸   a technical mistake: after a feint of the defender, the player in possession shoots ahead. A tackle is now possible;

▸   a tactical mistake: after one of the opponents (not in possession) has moved beyond the defenders, the players move up and mark the dribbler (covering the other defenders).

We have to remember that - by moving back near the goal - we can count on the goalkeeper, who can also send the ball away from the opponents.

In **diagram 16** A dribbles to the area vacated by 2 who is still in midfield. The defense line moves back and compacts. At this point the closest defender acts as if to move forward to challenge the dribble. A kicks the ball ahead and the defender comes out for a tackle, covered by the other two players. The variable is that one of the three front men (decided in advance) moves beyond the three defenders. Now the defender - who's able to see the others - calls out the marking and one player marks the dribbler while the other two cover. The exercise should be repeated with the ball on the right, left and center, always leaving out the equivalent defender.

1.11 Marking against crosses

This is a situation where the basic principles of marking have to be applied.
It's hard for the defender to see (when the cross is coming from deep up field) the player in possession and the opponent at the same time. Around the penalty area the marking is man-to-man. The marking duties can be exchanged only if the opposing player in possession gives us the time. The main points of this principle are:

▸ if there is time, the marking duties have to be passed to the next defender;

▸ if there is no time, man-to-man marking has to be applied.

In **diagram 17** A exchanges the marking duties with B (who does a feint to free himself from the marking). 3 closes B down as he's passing back to A. A serves A2 deep up field for a cross. Meanwhile the opposing forwards D, C and B move to the penalty area, man-to-man marked by 2,

Diagram 17

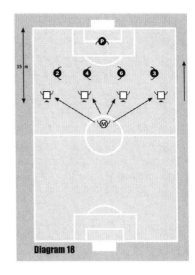

Diagram 18

16

4 and 6, while 3 acts as a shield without stopping A2 from crossing. The attackers have to score, the defenders have to block.

Very important: if you have to choose between seeing the player in possession and seeing the attacker, it's "better" not to see the ball. The reason is that the attacker is so close to the goal that you cannot let him free for any reason.

1.12   A few training exercises

4 v 4 + G with offside trap and counterattack **(diagram 18)**
The coach passes the ball to one of the 4 players to score a goal.
The defenders, when in possession of the ball, must dribble or receive in midfield without any block.
Variable: 5 v 4 + G a forward is added to the defensive line.
Variable: 6 v 4 + G two forwards are added to the defensive line.
Variable: repeat the three exercises starting with the defense placed just before midfield.

4 v 4 + G with one or more back-ups **(diagram 19)**
It's the same as in the previous exercise. But player A is placed behind the attackers' line - either close or far away - and able to move horizontally across the field. During the attack, player A can be served and he will decide to either take a long shot, a short pass or dribble back, to the right or to the left, able to see or not see the goal. The defense acts accordingly to these situations.
Variable: 5 v 4 + G a forward is added to the defensive line.
Variable: 6 v 4 + G two forwards are added to the defensive line. Note: the exercises practiced with the defensive line placed close to the penalty area can start with the goalkeeper (using his hands or his feet) sending the ball towards one of the attackers; in this way the defenders can get used to reacting to balls coming from behind.

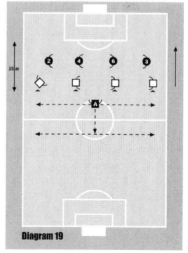

Diagram 19

4 v 3 + G with one player coming back, with offside trap and counterattack (**diagram 20)**

A starts dribbling and at the same time 2 comes back. The attackers have to score. The defenders, when in possession, have to lead or receive in midfield without the opponents blocking them. Repeat from all positions.

Variable: 4 v 3 + G without players coming back, with offside trap and counterattack

The difference is that 2 is not moving and not coming back. The 3 defenders accept the numerical inferiority and try to solve the situation.

Diagram 20

It's very important to alternate these situations with regular games where the teams or the positions are laid out, because there is always an alternation of the situations considered above. It is very helpful for the team training to recognize and solve these situations not only during their practice, but also in a global context.

Let's start fast

Walter Novellino is certainly one the emerging coaches of Italian soccer. His list of prizes won includes two promotions to Serie A with Venezia and Napoli. He also took Gualdo up to Serie C1 and almost to Serie B, but he lost the last game by penalties. Today he's again in Serie A with Piacenza. His specialty is 4:4:2 formation. Also, he's well known for his detailed work in the field and his effort to improve himself and the team.

Why 4:4:2?
First of all I must say that I prefer the 4:4:2 formation **(diagram 1)**. But with 4:4:2 the defenders can cover the whole field and make me feel safe. During the attack stage the 4 midfield players allow me to almost create a 4:2:4 formation. The 2 outer players must be complete players, very good in defense and attack. In fact, in my 4:4:2, they are the true attackers.

What do you expect from your team during the offensive stage?
I want the outer midfield players deep up field or the makeshift striker between midfield and the opposing defensive line. Again, I look for a deep play, not for a wide play.

But to do this you need enough space to start again…
In fact I never want the team to attack the opponents too "high", because if there isn't enough space, I cannot start again. If I don't do it this way, it's useless to have fast outer midfield players.

What if the opponents delay?
I try to leave them possession or to use my defenders to keep the ball behind and have the space to come out…

I can imagine what you'll try to do during the defensive stage….
Actually I have already answered. I don't want to win the ball too forward.

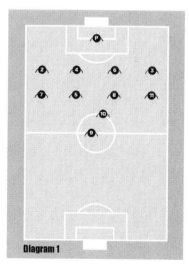

Diagram 1

But I want the players to be very fast when they start again.

When you have to create a team, what are the characteristics you look for in a single player and the different roles?

The central defenders must be very good in dribbling, but they also have to have great personality. I don't agree with those who say that the defenders must be fast at all costs. I had slow midfield players, but they were very fast and good in "understanding" all the different situations of the game. I choose the two backs keeping in mind that one player attacks more than the other. Usually the left back is the one pushing the most. The same happens with the center midfield players: one focuses more on quantity, the other on quality. As for the outer midfield players I have already described them when I explained the offensive stage. Regarding the 2 central midfield players I also want to say that they should always be staggered to have the chance to play deep and make space for receiving the ball where there are no opponents. I've already said that I prefer to play with one attacker and one player positioned in the final third behind the attacker. The attacker must be fast and must have a good technique. The player positioned in the final third moves on a semicircle, he should be fast, good in offensive 1 v 1 and able to play important long balls. These should be his characteristics.

It's fundamental that he never closes the spaces deep up field to the outer midfield players. Sometimes the player in the final third has to move behind the attacker to receive a back pass or he has to move centrally behind the attacker. I think it's very effective when he places himself between the defense and the opposing midfield area because he can easily receive and turn. On the other hand it's often difficult for the opposing teams to pass the marking duties and to find a clear way to neutralize him.

In general how do you organize the work during the offensive and defensive stages?

For the defensive stage I like to start from details. I analyze (with each position) all the situations we might have to face and then I transfer them into a regular game with a 11 v 11 situation. In that way I can always correct the mistakes.

For the offensive stage I don't believe in working with an 11 v 0 situation. It's not real. Instead, I like to challenge the players by analyzing the problems position by position. Then I transfer it all in a game and check the learning process.

How do you see the future of soccer?

I think it will be hard to impose a set game tactics because we all know each other and it's very difficult to surprise anyone anymore.

Tactics and feelings

Marcello Lippi is one of the most prepared coaches both in the national
and international scene. His career as a coach started with Carrarese,
Cesena and Lucchese. Then took off with Bergamo, Napoli, Inter and on
to great success with Juventus and the Italian national side.

His final year with Inter was considered by many people as a negative
experience, but it was actually the first step for rebuilding. Nevertheless,
Management decided to dismiss him.

Let's talk about 4:3:3 formation...

Well, before talking about tactics, I think we should say that the real
problem is in the mind. Talking about tactics is totally useless if the
mental attitude is wrong.

For instance...

A team has to have its own identity and game organization. All this has
to be mixed with humbleness and an inclination of the players to help
each other.

And 4:3:3...

It's a formation that I have used a lot during my career, but it's not the
only one. I think that each coach should be able to adopt several solutions during a game.

So...

For example, during my first year with Juventus, my 4: 3: 3 formation
included 3 forwards: Vialli, Ravanelli and Del Piero. Vialli and
Ravanelli are very strong, but not fast. So we were pressing the opponents high up-field to allow our forwards to start not too far away from
the opposing goal area. When I had fast players such as Boksic and
Padovano, or Inzaghi and Del Piero, together with Zidane, our purpose
was to pass the ball to these forwards as soon as possible.

What do you expect from your team during the offensive stage?

Everything depends on the characteristics of my attackers. I think it's
important to say something about it. Of course I have to give the team
some guidelines for the offensive maneuvers. But I can't expect the players to totally follow my guidelines during a game. When you're coaching

players like Zidane, Del Piero, Vieri etc…. you can't have them thinking that the score should come only in the way the coach wants!

On the other hand there could be some players who struggle to understand certain maneuvers. The role of the coach is to make things easy! This doesn't mean improvisation or confusion, but to find a balance between talent and organization of the game. I'd like to clarify that there are several kinds of 4:3:3 formation. There is the 4:3:3 formation with a center forward and 2 wide wings, the one with two forwards and a player positioned in the final third, the one with 3 tight forwards, etc….

What about your defensive stage…..

A basic principle says that you can't stay back with only two players. You can do it in a 2 v 2 situation, but I always want three players. Sometimes, if the backs have gone too far forward, the midfield player moves together with the defenders, becoming the third man. This happened at Juventus with Deschamps (**diagram 1**). And I saw it also with the Brazilian National Team (World Champion) in 1994.

And the two central defenders…?

I want them to be strong, fast and with good elevation.

What if they are slow?

I never had slow central players, but eventually we should exalt the quality of the position and the way it's organized. There should be more support for the two backs and we should try to create the offside trap because in this way we could cover a wide space against fast players.

You were talking about pressure during the attack….how do the forwards play in the 4:3:3 formation?

At the beginning with Juventus the 3 forwards would attack depending on their position when in possession. Del Piero would get back on the left wing, unless he was in a different position. Even if we could not attack in an organized way, the attackers would mark their direct opponent, up to the midfield line. This was giving a few more seconds to the team to take a good position. In **diagram 2** you see how the 3 forwards were attacking.

In **diagram 3** you see that you can neutralize possible shifts in the game with the action of the halfback.

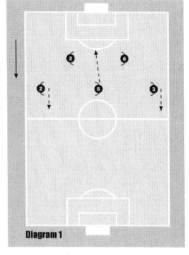

Diagram 1

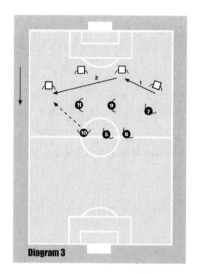

Diagram 2

Diagram 3

Did things change with Zidane's arrival?

Not at all. Zidane is a modern number ten. When he loses possession of the ball, he goes after his opponents. And he still has great technical qualities. Of course when Zidane was with me, I was using a 4: 3: 3 formation with him positioned behind the two forwards. And the French player was participating to win the ball back both through his personal availability to help the team and an amazing work ethic. Zidane would have gone back on the midfield line if his position was not allowing him to win the ball quickly.

How do you plan your work both during the defensive stage and the offensive stage?

In a very simple way. During the defensive stage I start analyzing (when necessary) the many possibilities I have. Then I translate them into a situation where there are some opponents. Finally I translate them into a game. During the offensive stage I offer some guidelines about solutions and maneuvers, keeping in mind what the opponents' layout is. Here too, I follow the methodology mentioned above for the defensive stage. But with Juventus - especially from the third year, when we had established our identity - I was using many theme games (**diagrams 4, 5 and 6**) to practice the two stages. I have two purposes:

▸ to motivate my players;
▸ not to annoy them with exercises regarding things they already know very well and have practiced a lot.

Finally, what does Marcello Lippi think about the future of soccer?

I think the future of soccer dwells in discovering the limit where you

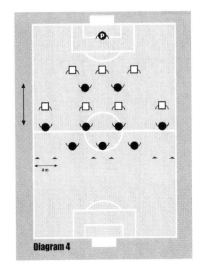

Diagram 4

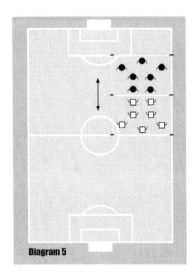

Diagram 5

obtain the necessary organization without changing the quality and the characteristics of a player.

Diagram 4: a game with 7 players (3 defenders and 4 midfield players, plus the goalkeeper); with 9 or 8 attackers who must score.

If the 7 players win the ball back, they have to start again and try to score through the goals positioned beyond the midfield line.

Of course depending on the purpose, the team will have to be laid out with a defending formation or with an attacking formation.

Also, if the purpose is to attack, you can position your defense accordingly to what you think your opponents will do.

Diagram 5: in a game with a 7 v 7 situation, if you want to work on the two forwards and the midfield player (during the offensive stage) functioning as a final third player, the teams should be positioned with a 3:2:2 formation. The width of the field can also be covered by the outer players. In this game the position can be taken by the backs or by the outer midfield players.

Diagram 6: a game with a 3 v 3 to continue the training for closing down the player in possession and for covering.

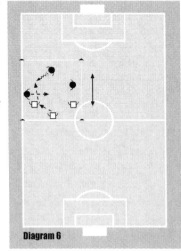

Diagram 6

24

2.1 Midfield with 4 players

The analysis of the defensive problems of a midfield line with 4 players is not very different from the problems of a defensive line with 4 players. The first thing we have to look at is the cover of the opposing player in possession. We have to make clear that since we are talking about the midfield line, we can't use the offside trap. We position ourselves on one cover line and we use the methodology of a line with 4 players.

If the dribbler cannot see, the midfield player will be placed further up-field, ready to press. If the dribbler is able to see, he will be more covered. The same happens when it's necessary to exchange marking duties and back-ups to neutralize the opposing diagonal movements, triangles and overlapping.

When we have to solve the problem of deep shots, it's enough to add the midfield position to our defense. During long shots, the midfield players move back facing the defenders and try to receive the ball from them. The very same happens when we talk about passing the ball back.

On the other hand, when we are dealing with penetrating passes, the opposing forwards have the chance to either:

▶ receive the ball on the defensive line or
▶ receive the ball in front of the midfield line.

In this case we will have an exchange of positions and the defender will go with the attacker to the midfield player. The defender will inform the midfield player about the opponent's arrival, pass the marking duties and go back to his position.

Very important: the defender should call the midfield player by his name. It's not enough to say "coming", because the midfield player is turning his back and can't see what is happening.

A numerical inferiority or a wrong position should be analyzed in the same way as a defense with 4 players. If we analyze the marking against crosses, we could add 2 midfield players to control (man-by-man) the two opposing midfield players.

2.2   Midfield with 3 or 5 players

Midfield with 3 players
The reader will be able to understand the following principles and exercises very easily. It's all about the position taken when we close down a lateral ball **(diagram 21)** and a central ball **(diagram 22)**.

Midfield with 5 players
In this case as well, we propose only a few maneuvers which are important when we have a midfield with 5 players. **Diagram 23** shows the marking of a lateral ball. **Diagram 24** shows the marking of a central ball.

2.3   Doubling teaming

An important aspect of an organized defensive stage is doubling of the marking. In other words, when two players move against an opponent. In this way we create double teaming pairs between the defenders and the midfield players, who change depending on the formation used:

▶   midfield with 4 players **(diagram 25)**: 2 doubles up with 8, 5 with 4, 10 with 6 and 7 with 3;
▶   midfield with 3 players **(diagram 26)**: 8 doubles up with 2, 5 with 4 and 10 with 3;
▶   midfield with 5 players: just like the situation mentioned above, but with 7 and 11 cutting off the back pass.

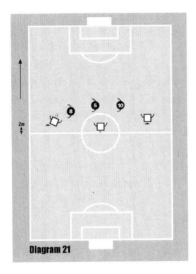

Diagram 21

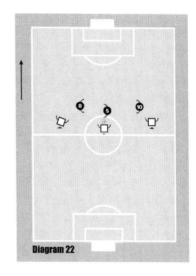

Diagram 22

Very important: if the opponent can see the goal, when 8 moves to double up, he should mark towards the inside of the player in possession; 2 should mark the outside of the player in possession **(diagram 26b)**.
If the player in possession cannot see the goal, 8 is placed behind him and 2 is in front.
2 marks the player in possession and prevents him from turning around. 8 challenges him **(diagram 26c)**. The two defenders can't be too spread out, otherwise the opponent can sneak in and move away.
The doubling of the marking should happen between players of different

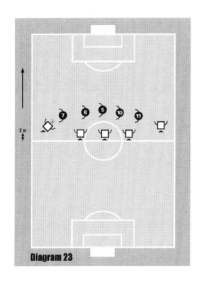

Diagram 23

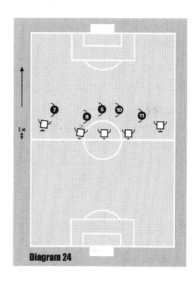

Diagram 24

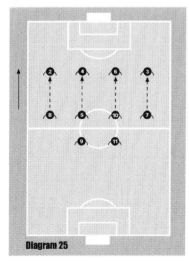

Diagram 25

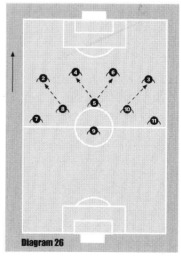

Diagram 26

27

lines (defense and midfield). In this way we would avoid uncovering a single position. But if we can't avoid such a situation, then we should do it only when in case of numerical superiority of the defenders.

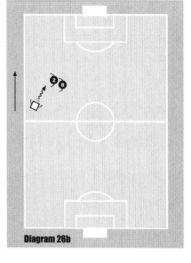

2.4 Position with 2, 1 or 3 forwards

Position with 2 forwards
You can see the attackers positioned in such a way in the 4:4:2 formation, in the 4:3:1:2 formation or in the 4:4:1:1 formation, where - during the defensive stage - the player positioned in the final third is doubling up with the other forward.

In each formation the marking phase changes depending on what each coach thinks and, most of all, on the opponents' layout. So we will explain the basic principles only.

The two forwards act as a shield and have to prevent the defenders from placing themselves vertically in the center. When they have to face two central defenders, one of them covers and the other closes the defenders down **(diagram 27)**.

If the ball moves to the side, the closest forward takes position to prevent

Diagram 26c

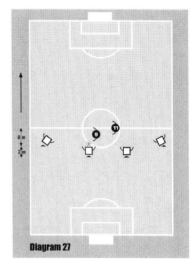

Diagram 27

28

the player receiving the ball from passing back. The other forward, instead,
moves to cover (diagram 27b).
It's obvious that when the opposing
defense has 3 players, we will have to
analyze and eventually solve the numerical inferiority. There are some coaches
who accept numerical inferiority and try
to address the game to the side and start
a real marking phase.

Diagram 27b

Position with 1 or 3 forwards
Here we talk about formations such as
4:3:3, 4:2:1:3 or 4:5:1 where, with a
single central forward, we will always
experience numerical inferiority. And in
case of a defense with 3 players, we will
even have a double inferiority.
Here it's true what we have said in the paragraph above: some coaches
solve the numerical inferiority by passing the marking duties to the midfield players; some others delay and try to send the ball towards the
outer lines, where - since the opposition cannot move at 360° - the pressing is easier.
For instance, let's consider the problem with a 4:3:3 formation against 4
defenders. In this situation 9 can "dance" between B and C without
engaging in a tackle with 7 and 11, who are blocking and marking A and

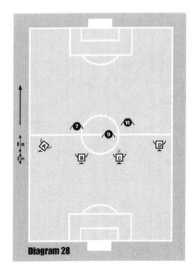

Diagram 28

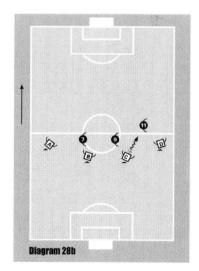

Diagram 28b

D (backs).

When C or B are oriented toward the outside, the block can begin (**see diagram 28 and 28b**), with 9 closing C (player in possession) and 7 and 11 marking and blocking near the ball. Vice versa some coaches propose the following blocks:

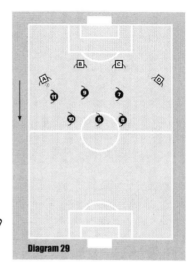

▸ A in possession (**diagram 29**): 11 comes out, 9 covers and marks, 7 covers and marks, 10 and 5 are near the ball and 8 focuses on game shifts;

▸ C in possession (**diagram 30**): 9 comes out, 11 and 7 cover and mark, 10 and 5 are near the ball and 8 focuses on game shifts;

Diagram 29

▸ B in possession (**diagram 31**): 7 comes out, 9 and 11 mark and cover, 8 and 5 are near the ball and 10 focuses on game shifts;

▸ D in possession (**diagram 32**): 7 comes out, 11 and 9 mark and cover, 8 and 5 are near the ball and 10 focuses on game shifts.

It's clear that in these situations we don't accept the numerical inferiority, but we try to solve it by being active without waiting for the opponents to make their moves.

In diagram 32 we notice that back D can receive the ball forward as well

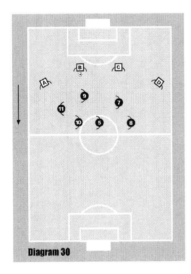

Diagram 30

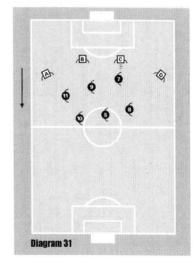

Diagram 31

as square. Here we risk the midfield player reaching the ball before the back, who is moving forward.

Some coaches use their back player in this proactive way to neutralize the numerical superiority of the opponents.

2.5   Analysis of the team behaviors

During the consideration of a defensive methodology it is good to look at:

▶   learning of individual defensive basic principles;
▶   learning of position and team tactics.

Some coaches like to start from the details and then continue gradually towards the general aspects. Others begin from the team and move on with the individuals.

We should respect both visions and remember that when we are dealing with young beginners it is good to build the player and this is why we focus more on the individual aspects.

We don't want to repeat the team exercises we have already looked at, but there are a few of them we'd like to consider one more time **(diagram 33)**.

The 4 players in line work as landmarks. The coach challenges each one of them, pretending to be in possession of the ball; the team starts moving with the 4 defenders marking the two forwards (A and B) and the two backs reducing the distance (depending on the position of the ball) from one of the cones representing a wide opponent.

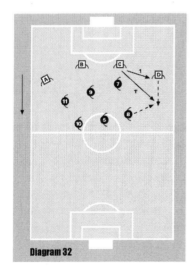

Diagram 32

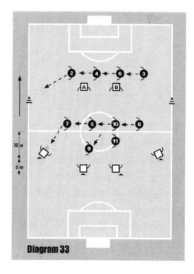

Diagram 33

31

There is the variable of the 4 players passing the ball to each other; then we add the chance for the player in possession to see or not to see. In this way the different positions will train:

▶ the forwards and the defenders to be more aggressive, or - on the other hand - to focus on the cover;

▶ the defenders to correctly relate to each other for the marking of the forwards and of the wide opponent.

In diagram 33 we look at the 4:4:2 formation just as an example. Also the exercises regarding the neutralization of the shots, the penetrating passes or the back passes can be proposed again with the defensive methodology or with defense plus midfield. Of course we should also add the forwards.

Then we can integrate all this with a tactical offensive work. In other words, after playing the ball back or after the marking, we can trigger some offensive restarts depending on the formation or on the strategy we have to face.

As a general principle, we will keep in mind that on a change of possession:

▶ the defense can send the ball back to the midfield players who have the chance to play it, otherwise the midfield players are marked and receive assistance from the defenders coming from the back;

▶ the midfield players are supported by the defenders who have to move ahead towards the forwards since there are no covers available nearby;

▶ the defense can control and play   short balls from the back;

▶ the defense can control and   move ahead.

This principle is valid for any defensive exercise, either by man, by position or by team. It's the counterattack concept. The action doesn't end with possession of the ball!

There are many teams that are well organized for the defensive stage; but the situation changes when they get possession of the ball. Once the players have digested the general principles of attack and defense, they should get used to a defense always ready to restart immediately.

When we talk about organization we are referring both to the defensive and to the offensive stage. The problem is not about what we want to do, but about doing it well. It's not about man marking or zone marking, but about playing well.

As you can see we did not overwhelm with too many exercises. We have preferred to use them to explain the defensive principles of the single player, of the position and of the team. It's useless for the coach to know a lot of exercises if he doesn't know their purpose or the principles of the game. In such case he would not know what to correct and how.

The exercises should come from the knowledge of the coach and should be easily created by him. In fact it's a mistake to look at the training sections of famous coaches and "copy" their work. The skill is about adapting to your reality what you have seen. What we have learned from others should inspire us to create something on "our own".

We would need a revolutionary

The journey of Carlo Ancelotti as a coach began as Arrigo Sacchi's assistant in the national team. In the 1995-96 season he was responsible of his own team for the first time. At that time Ancelotti was coaching Reggiana and he was immediately promoted to Serie A. During the two following seasons he worked with Parma. In 1998-99, in February, he went to Juventus, taking the place of Marcello Lippi.

What about 4:3:1:2 formation.....?

It's the formation we use with Juventus (**diagram 1**), but it has to be adapted so that we can exploit the skills of each player.

Why do you use it?

Because it's a formation that allows us to cover the wings with the players and not in a static way as we did last year. In fact, last year our game was more static and we had the tendency to center the game. Today we can be less predictable on the wings and alternate a lateral game to a central game.

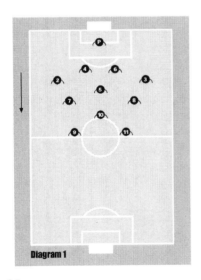

Diagram 1

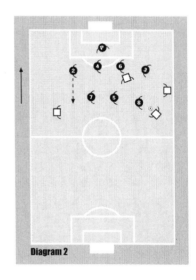

Diagram 2

34

What's the advantage?

As I've said before, the lateral wings are covered in a dynamic way because during the attacking stage there aren't static positions.

What are the problems?

Sometimes it's hard to close down the wings and to play as the fifth man during the defensive stage.

This might create some problems during the fast changes of game...

Of course. But if the back player doesn't have a man to mark, he can come out on the midfield players (**diagram 2**), otherwise he stays together with the defenders. If the opposing midfield player is way behind, he'll get cover by one of our midfield players. If the opposing midfield player stays ahead, then he'll be covered by our back player.

Do you let the makeshift striker come between the three midfield players?

No, because I think that we should ask for long runs from the makeshift strikers during the defensive stage. But it's obvious that they also have to be included in the defensive action.

How?

If the opponents have a defense with three men (**diagram 3**), the final third player marks the central defender and the two forwards move towards the other two opposing defenders. If the opponents defend with four men, the makeshift striker closes (during a lateral pass) down the opposing midfield player near the ball (**diagram 4**).

What are the themes you follow during the attacking stage?

The width of the field has to be taken by the two backs, who must have

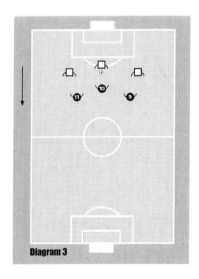

Diagram 3

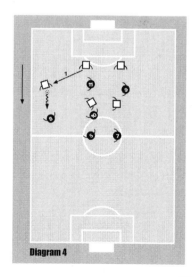

Diagram 4

offensive skills. This is true also for the lateral midfield players, who must be able to move. If neither the backs nor the midfield players can control the width of the field, one of the two forwards will guarantee the control while a player positioned in the final third will move next to the other forward to reassemble the position (**diagram 5**). We must say that when the ball is in our half of the field, our "director" is the player positioned in front of defense, whereas in the other half of the field it's the makeshift striker who has to be seen. The reason is that with this formation the player in front of the defense has defensive duties and must help to build the game from the back. Unlike the two lateral midfield players he doesn't move forward too much. He has to take advantage of the characteristics of the makeshift striker he's playing with.

What are these characteristics?

As usual, technical qualities (especially in offensive 1 v 1 situations) and tactical qualities, such as the ability of playing penetrating balls and playing between the midfield line and the opposing defense. I also want to say that I prefer (as many other coaches) to have a fast forward, whereas the other is strong physically.

What if we reverse the problem and we have to face a makeshift striker...

If we play with four players in the back, one of them will focus primarily on the defensive stage. If we play with 3 players, our central defender could play with a 1 v 1 situation.

How do you develop defensive and offensive themes during training?

I use a progression by position and then I expand the defensive stage with the opponents active most of the time. The reason is that the players know all the secrets.

As for the attacking stage I let the theme develop when we are in a situation of numerical superiority. In fact, in this case, I don't agree with those who say that the formation is a limitation.

Why is that?

Because a coach has to say which kinds of movements he wants and should give clear indications. These are "guides" for the talent, but it will be up to the talent to enrich the situation. But a "guide" is always necessary. As for the

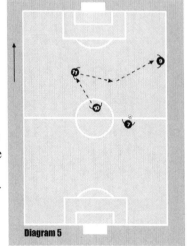

Diagram 5

work we do weekly, I must say that now I don't work so much by position. During one exercise I tend to unite two positions, both in the defensive and offensive stage.

Do you think it's useful to vary the formation during a match?
Only if the team has the knowledge to do it. Of course if you have to move from 4:3:1:2 formation to 4:4:2 formation, it's not a problem. Otherwise I think it's better to avoid any improvisation.

How do you see the future of soccer?
There is less space to move for everyone. The teams have a very well organized defensive stage. In Italy we play a kind of soccer where we like to limit more than create. To play differently we should take some pressure off the coaches. The quality of the coaches is very good, but we don't always have the chance to work for a long period. To change this thing it would be necessary to find a revolutionary.

Returning to technique

Mauro Sandreani began his career in Perugia where he worked as assistant coach. Then he moved to Padova and stayed there for 7 years; for the first two seasons he worked again as assistant coach, but towards the end of the third season he became the head coach and saved the team from going down. The following year (still in Serie B) he ended the season gaining the fifth place and almost winning promotion to Serie A. The next season (1993-94), thanks to a player named Del Piero, he took Padova to Serie A after 32 years. Then we saw him in Torino and Ravenna (Serie B), Empoli (Serie A) and in Tenerife, Spain. Nowadays, as he's waiting for his own team, he's a very good TV commentator.

Why should a coach choose the 4:2:3:1 formation?

Because with everyone using the 4:4:2 formation, it has become predictable. This other formation gives you the chance to better characterize the 4:4:2 formation. In fact the 4:2:3:1 formation embodies the advantage of a defense with 4 players - that I consider the safest - together with the cover of the two central halfbacks.

Also, unlike 4:4:2, in this case we can use the fantasy of one or two makeshift strikers because with this formation we have at our disposal one forward and three makeshift strikers.

Three makeshift strikers?

Absolutely. Look at France National Team **(diagram 1)** where Anelka was playing as forward and Zidane behind him together with Dugarry, Gjorkaeff or Henry on the outer side; two lateral players and one player positioned on the final third. Also Portugal National did it during the European Championship laying out Nuno Gomes as forward, Rui Costa behind and Figo, Joao, Pinto or Conceicao on the out-

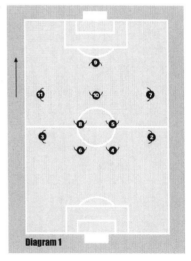

Diagram 1

side. The option is that you always have 4 attackers.

It's also a formation easy to modify...

Yes, because you just need to lower the wings and you obtain a 4:4:1:1. Or you can bring the wings up to have a 4:2:1:3.

With this formation, what do you do when in possession?

It depends on the skills of the players. In Spain, where they were playing a lot in this way, there was Valencia with a forward like Claudio Lopez and two outer players very good in moving deep. Real Madrid, having very good dribblers, could organize a game focused on horizontal possession, since on the outer side there were players very capable in the 1 v 1 offensive situation.

During the defensive stage it could happen that you only have 6 players to defend...

I think it's acceptable. It's obvious that this formation favors taking time rather than high pressing, because - playing with 4 attackers deep upfield - we are often in a bad position and we have to slow down in order to move back to defend ourselves and allow the forwards to get back in position. In this situation the role of the two midfield players for slowing down the game and protecting the defense is very important.

What about the two midfield players....

We would lay out two "hammers", but in Spain - for instance - one of them (sometimes even both of them) is a geometric player. In fact I saw Redondo playing very well there.

During the attack what do you ask of the 4 players ahead?

To participate in the defensive stage. In fact they could lay out the 3 players of the final third behind the forward. But in this case they must have the support of a well organized defense and they must be very active without exaggerating. On a lateral ball I always ask number 10 to move on the first opposing back up; I ask 9 to "dance" between the two or three opposing defenders. I ask 7 and 11 to get back on the external players. As you can see it's nothing terrible. Also, I keep in mind that, upon losing possession of the ball they are all "mixed up", each player will get back to a zone where he can quickly consolidate his position, even if it's not the same as in the beginning.

Speaking about the characteristics of the players, you did not say anything about the forward and the 4 defenders yet...

9 has to have strength and height: beside being heavily built, he has to be able to move to create the space that will be attacked from the back. In my opinion the best in this role is Morientes. The 4 players in the back must be specialized in this formation and must be very keen during the

defensive stage. I think the two backs participate in the attack - with the addition of spaces created by the diagonal movements of 7 and 11 - only till the midfield line. After that it seems to be too much, since I already have 4 attackers!

So again the 4:2:3:1....

This formation combines several possibilities in the offensive stage: the wings cutting in as in the 4:3:3 formation, 1 v 1 solution on the outer player and the theme of the third man. Remember that both France and Spain mix the numerical superiority with the quality of the players in the 1 v 1 situation, not only

Diagram 2

with paying attention to the movements. Remember that unlike Italy - where in Serie A we play with 7 or 8 different formations, in Spain they either use this formation or the 4:3:1:2. Nobody plays with a defense with 3 players anymore. During the last European Cup, 12 teams out of 16 were playing with a defense with 4 players.

Could you show us some offensive themes?

In **diagram 2** you can see 11 serving 9, while 9 - with the support of 10 - continues the action for the diagonal movement of 7. In **diagram 3**, 9 can

Diagram 3

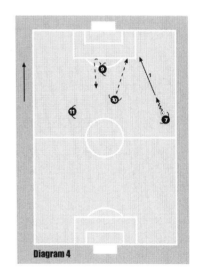

Diagram 4

play deep and facilitates the insertion of 10 from behind. And finally **(diagram 4)** 10 cuts in behind the opposing back, with 9 receiving short.

What do you think we will see in the future?

Soccer needs to go back to the technical basic principles. It's hard to find a 2 v 1 situation through movements. It's better to work with quality (1 v 1 situation) through good training. We should also encourage the creativity of the players. Soccer can't abandon fantasy and technical quality.

3.1 In-depth disposition, upward movement, width, mobility and unpredictability

Before looking at the details, it would be good to briefly consider the principles that a team should apply to have an effective attacking stage. In order to have a correct attack, these requirements have to be respected.

In-depth disposition: the action to elude the marking should never happen in line with the player in possession. In the case of two unmarked players, we should try to create a triangle (of any kind) with the player in possession. When two players come from the same position, they have to respect the principle of "opposite depths" (meaning long and short, inside and outside, etc.)

Upward movement: it's always better to arrive as fast as possible toward the opponents' goal. Between the several options for passing the ball, it's better to play on the teammate who is further ahead.

Width: during the offensive stage we should try to use the entire width of the field, including the area opposite to the ball, in case it's not possible to move ahead in the game zone.

Mobility: without moving it's difficult to maintain possession. To move with only one player is not enough, because we would be predictable. We have to move with several players and create several situations for the player in possession. The players in possession could:

▸ come in with a feint before the movement to elude the marking;
▸ come in with a diagonal run;
▸ come in with a run with a change of direction;
▸ come in with an overlapping run (to create a 2 v 1 situation);
▸ come in with opposite depths (as we said for the In-depth disposition).

Unpredictability: a talented player always puts something of his own in a project. Soccer is a game of situations that have to be "read" carefully. The true "fantasy" is that which allows you to choose the most effective solution. Dribbling - for instance - is effective, if it's just one of the many choices that the player in possession has. But if it's the only choice, then it shows that the game is not organized. It's obvious that we cannot leave ignore the individual quality of our attackers, which has to be mixed with organization.

In the past, soccer was based mostly on the individual qualities of the players. Then, with the advent of Arrigo Sacchi and the wrong interpretation of his method, we have thought that only organization was important. The single player wasn't worthy anymore. But we think that the future of soccer is in what we have said above: organization and talent mixed in the same game context.

3.2 Layout from behind with a defense with 4,3 or 5 players

Defense with 4 players
Assuming that it's possible to start the game with an action of the defenders from behind, let's see how the situation could unfold. In case of a central defender (**diagram 34**) capable to see the goal, the back player moves and receives into space. 4 and 6 guarantee the cover in case the player should loose possession. In the next situation (**diagram 35**), 2 is closed down and passes to the central defender 4, who then passes to the back 3 on the other side. In case 4 is unable to shoot, he can be backed up by the other central (6) who will be in charge of passing the ball. After the situation shown in diagram 35, it could happen that the defenders cannot pass the ball to one another nor can they be backed up by the

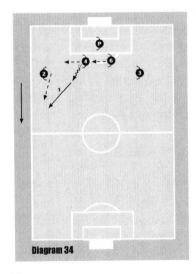

Diagram 34

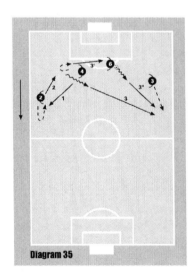

Diagram 35

44

midfield players. In such a case the defenders must pass long to the forwards.

"If you are closed down, bypass". Of course it doesn't mean to kick randomly, but to get organized in order to face any situation (diagram 36).

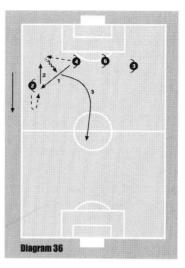

Diagram 36

Let's consider two other solutions, where we see the insertion of the two central defenders 4 and 6. I don't know how doable these solutions are, because in the midfield area there are always several opposing players. But it's good to consider and remember these solutions. In **diagram 37** we can see that the central defender 4 has the chance to play forward. The other central player (6) moves forward either to receive or to create space for the midfield player who's coming short to receive the ball. Then 4 covers and provides back up. The situation is different in **diagram 38**, where 2 has received the ball from the goalkeeper and the central defender 4 moves forward, while 6 covers.

Defense with 3 players

The basic concepts are the very same: the two backs broaden up together with the central player 5, who is ready to cover (**diagram 39**). It doesn't

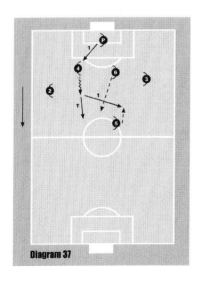

Diagram 37

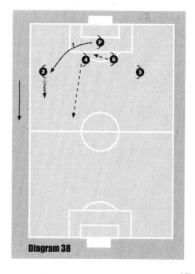

Diagram 38

change much if it's 5 to start the action, receiving the ball from the goalkeeper (**diagram 40**).

Defense with 5 players
In this case also it's almost the same. Of course the cover (in case we lose possession) is guaranteed by 5 players. In **diagram 41** we see the backs 2 and 6 broadening, with the central players 3 and 4 covering and supporting from behind, together with the central defender 5.

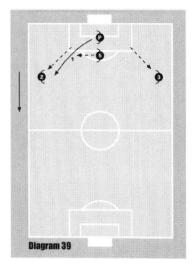

Diagram 39

3.3 Midfield with 4,3 or 5 players

Midfield with 4 players
The midfield position with 4 players - accompanied by a 4 player defense - is very different from the same position with a 3 player defense. This depends on the fact that in the first case the two lateral midfield players can be assisted (during the defensive stage) by the two backs. In case of a defense with 3 players, this can't be done.
It's clear that in this case the outer players have to be strong because they have to cover a bigger distance.
In **diagram 42** we see some situations that could happen: we are in pos-

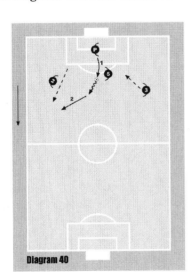

Diagram 40

Diagram 41

46

session of the ball on the right wing, the midfield player 5 moves behind the player in possession to support him, trying to stay in a position where he can see the field as much as possible. The other central player (10) moves slightly forward, acting as a final third player, and he's ready to take advantage of the space created by the attacker **(diagram 43)**. It could happen that 10 is marked and to free himself he must exchange position with the midfield player 8 on the left wing **(diagram 44)**. It's obvious that if 5 is attacked by the opponents, 10 will move to help him. Another option could be that 5 moves

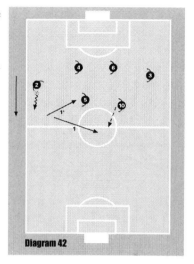

Diagram 42

forward to make space for 10 to receive the ball and decide what to do. We have an alternative to these movements when the ball is central. It's possible to exchange positions between the two midfield players to make space for receiving the ball **(diagram 44b)**.

Midfield with 3 players
The midfield position with 3 players involves a player in the back called "center back of the method" since with his feints and skills he reminds us of the center half of the "method": the game formation with which in the

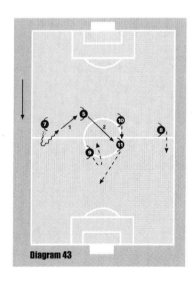

Diagram 43

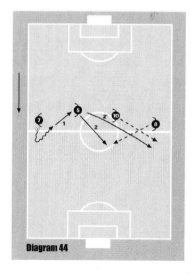

Diagram 44

47

30s' Italy won everything.

The other two lateral midfield players can have different characteristics of quality, quantity etc… The player of the method is the leader of the maneuver. He is the one in charge of turning the ball, cuts in centrally and supports the possession of the ball.

In **diagram 45** we see that 5 was able to receive the ball thanks to the space opened by 10. Later on also the other halfback 8 can spread his position. If 5 can't receive the ball, but needs to move deep to unmark himself, he will use the space created by 8 with his movement toward the center (**diagram**

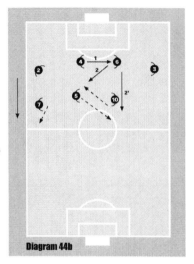

Diagram 44b

46). If 5 is unable to receive the ball - often the opponents press him- we have to find another solution as in **diagram 47**, where the central defender in possession (2) moves in deep, helped by the space opened by 8 cut-

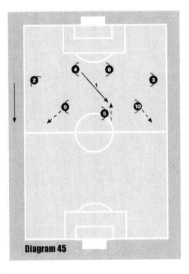

Diagram 45

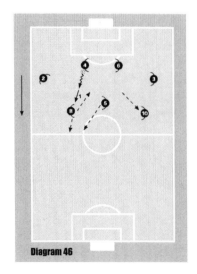

Diagram 46

ting in.

Midfield with 5 players

We can repeat the concepts expressed
for the midfield position with 3 and 4
players. If the fifth player is in line with
the other 4 players, we will have a situation similar to the midfield position
with 3 players, but with the addition of
the two lateral players on the wings
(diagram 48). On the other hand, if the
fifth player is a makeshift striker, the
midfield with 4 players will use this
new man to vary the offensive stage
(diagram 49).

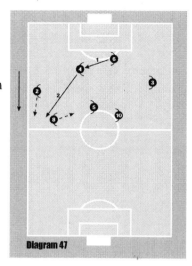

Diagram 47

3.4 Attack with 2 or 3 forwards

Attack with 2 forwards

Before showing some examples of offensive solutions, we would like to
clarify the principles that rule these movements. It's obvious that the first
player to act is the one nearest the ball, while the other player follows.
When we talk about these two players we mean that one plays as referring forward and the other as final third player.

Let's take a look at **diagram 50**:

5 is in possession. 9 acts first, he moves forward and then deep up-field.

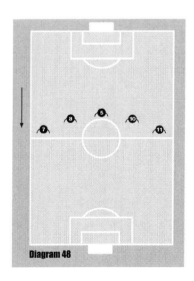

Diagram 48

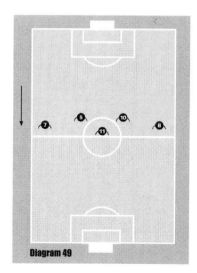

Diagram 49

49

11, on the other hand, moves back and gives support so that 10 can let 8 move in deep. Then 8 crosses to the far post thanks to the two forwards (9 and 11) and the midfield player (5).

One variable is represented in diagram 50; 11 closes the triangle with 9 who is completing the action. You can see another solution in **diagram 51**: 9 moves toward 5 and the center. 11 moves in at first and then he moves away.

It's clear that the two players move always opposing each other, one comes and the other goes, one moves in and the other moves out, and so on... This allows the player in possession to have two different choices.

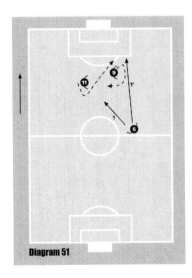

Diagram 50

Attack with 3 forwards

In this case too we have to make a distinction between teams laying out three forwards, two wings and one central attacker and teams laying out two forwards and a final third player behind them.

The coach should know the principles that rule the movements; the player near the ball is the first one to move, starting the rotation of the other two players.

In **diagram 52** (2 forwards and 1 makeshift striker), we see 5 in posses-

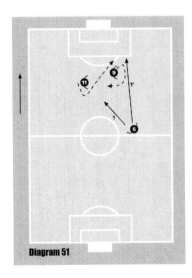

Diagram 51

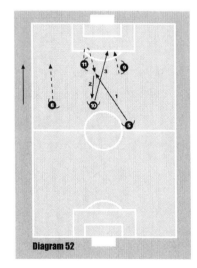

Diagram 52

sion; 11 moves towards him and then 10 serves and supports 9 deep.

In **diagram 53** (3 forwards) we have 8 serving 9, who's moving on to 7. 7 can serve:

▸ the diagonal movement in of 11;
▸ the insertion of 3 in the space created by the diagonal movement in of 11.

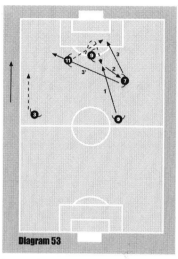

There are some interesting solutions that might happen in a midfield area with three players, with a vertex; when this player is added to the other 3 forwards.

In **diagram 54** we see the center forward 9 receiving after a penetrating movement, with which 10 is supported, as 8 and 5 are in the back. The left wing 11 cuts in, with 3 in open space. In **diagram 55** the central insertion comes from 10, after an exchange between 9 and 7.

More complicated is the solution in **diagram 56**, where 9 receives the support from the two central midfield players for the diagonal movement of one of the two wings. But we have to clarify that depending on the different formations, there will be a lot of variation in the functions and the skills of the positions and the players who are part of them.

Following we can see all the cases where a midfield with three players -

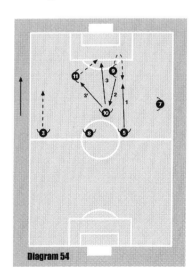

Diagram 54

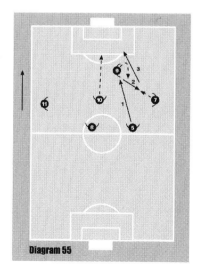

Diagram 55

depending on the formation - requires different skills.

4: 3: 3   The 3 midfield players have to cover a large section of the field and they can't always count on the support of the wings. For this reason we will ask for complementary players to make a defensive "sacrifice".

5: 3: 2   The 3 midfield players receive support from the two backs for covering the wings. So they only have to worry about covering the central space. They can have different characteristics and duties.

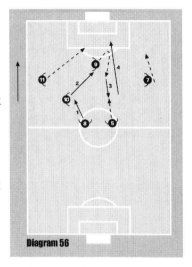

Diagram 56

3: 3: 1: 3 In this case the 3 defenders and the 3 midfield players have to take care of the defense only. Eventually they can create the action from behind.

On the other hand, when we talk about midfield with 4 players, we see that:

4: 4: 2   The two external midfield players can be less complementary compared to a 3: 4: 3 or a 3: 4: 1: 2 formation because they are protected by the two backs behind them. The two central midfield players will never be in a situation of external overlapping, but will work to keep the ball moving or for a central insertion.

Depending on the formation, the unfolding of the maneuver can vary, as well as the attackers' characteristics. It's clear that each coach, knowing these principles, will modify the game organization to fit the characteristics of the players at his disposal. Depending on the formation, the action to win possession of the ball could be as follows:

4: 3: 3   The central forward (often with his back to the goal) will function as a wall pass and then serve the diagonal movement of the wings, or will back up another player to allow him to pass back to another teammate or to serve the insertions into the space created by the wings. The feature of this formation will be the wings cutting in and the subsequent insertions.

4: 3: 1: 2 or 3: 4: 1: 2 With two forwards and one makeshift striker the ball will have to move on the ground, looking for lateral movements more than anything else. The makeshift striker will have to move along the offensive line and try to find the best position to use his own skills or to take advantage of the position where the opponent is weaker.

3: 3: 1: 3 With this formation we look for depth on the central forward, on the wings or on the player positioned in the final third. We also include the defenders.

4: 4: 2 In this case the two backs are not very strong in a defensive 1 v 1 situation, because the outer midfield player can often move to help them. When we have a 4: 3: 3 formation the situation is different because the doubling up of the midfield players can't always be punctual. In other words, they must be stronger when in a 1 v 1 situation. In addition to this, since the action starts from behind, the backs must cover the width of the field, whereas in a 4: 4: 2 formation we have two wide midfield players.

3: 4: 1: 2, 3: 4: 3 or 3: 3: 1: 3 In case of formations with 3 defenders, their characteristics are mostly defensive because they will have to build the game from the back or they will have to make long passes to the forwards.

We also have to remember that - in order to complete this analysis - there aren't defensive or offensive formations as such, but there are attitudes and behaviors of the team with which each formation receives the special touch of the coach.

I start from four players

Maurizio Viscidi is one of the most prepared young coaches (born in 1962) of Italian soccer. He started with the junior teams of Padova and Milan and won the Championship coaching players like Del Piero and Sartor. Then he started with the first team in Casarano (C1), two years in Lodigiani (C1), in Pescara (B), Viterbese (C1) and then Lucchese (C1).

I'd like to speak with you about 4:2:1:3 formation...

Fine, but I think we talk too much about numbers! For instance, I believe that when we talk about defense we should not talk about 3 or 5 players.

What do you mean?

The most important thing is how many players I place behind the ball line during the defensive stage. So it doesn't make sense to talk about 4:3:3, if the two wings run after the ball. In such case we should talk about 4:5:1 and so on.

Why do you prefer the formations with 4 players in defense?

Because with 4 defenders you are depending less on the opponents: you cover the opponents' offensive line. With a defense with 3 players you can't do this; you only have the 3 central players and it works only if the opponents are playing with two central forwards. For example, if the opponents play with a central forward and the other forward is behind the outer midfield player, I will be in trouble...

But formations with 4 defenders have problems of central 2 v 2 situation...

If the two forwards are on the side of the ball, the 2 v 2 situation is accepted with two cover lines (**diagram 1**); if one of the two forwards stays wider, I leave him to the back because the 2 v 2 situation is accepted in narrow spaces (**diagram 2**).

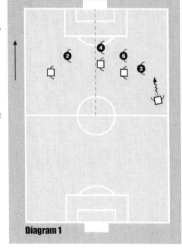

Diagram 1

Let's go back to the first question...
In the 4:2:1:3 situation (**diagram 3**) the
two midfield players have classical
duties as in the 4:4:2. The problem
stands for the two external players (7 and
11) who will have to:

▸   play as wings during the attack;
▸   play as fourth and third, or even
        fifth, midfield players during
        the defensive stage.

A bit too much...
10 has to have the typical characteristics
of a player in the final third - while 9 is
movable and capable of receiving the
ball - he should act as a wall pass, main-

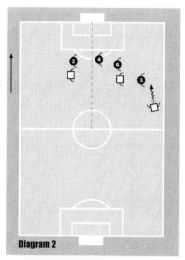

Diagram 2

tain possession and be strong. 10 doesn't attack too deep because he is
the only central forward and would get too far away from the other players. This formation is effective only when playing in the opponents' half
of the field because 7 and 11 can get back only on the midfield players
and not on the defenders.

What's your action for winning possession of the ball?
Let's pretend that 2 is in possession (**diagram 4**), the opponent A gets on
2 while A1 blocks the ball from going deep towards 9: in such a situation
we will keep the ball moving, passing to 5 and then to 8. In the following situation (**diagram 5**), A2 closes 5 down so that:

Diagram 3

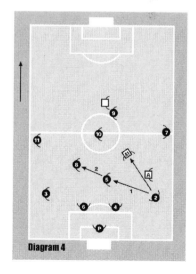

Diagram 4

- I can ask for a change of position between 5 and 8 to elude the marking and receive;
- or I can pass to 9 moving to the side.

When the ball is passed to 9, 7 moves to receive towards the inside since (**diagram 6**) generally the defender tends to run to cover the player who is coming out on 9. In case we come out on the halfbacks, it could happen that:

- if 5 is in possession and 7 receives from behind the defender, 5 will play and cross between the defenders' back and the goal line for the insertion of 9, 10 and 11;
- if 7 receives the ball cutting from inside, 9 cuts in as well, 10 goes straight and 11 moves toward the inside; if 7 receives the ball at his feet and he is in a 1 v 1 situation and he wins this situation going in and out, then the above situations will repeat themselves. I also think it would be good to reverse the wings only (the right wing to the left and vice versa) and not the external midfield players (4:4:2 and so on…).

During the defensive stage there could be some problems to find the position of the body. I also want to say that with this formation - since there are 4 supporters positioned in front - the two backs usually don't move much or they do, only if I have tall players in front and able to cross pass.

The two backs move only if 7 and 11 cut in trying to make space, or 7 and 11 can turn around and serve 2 and 3 overlapping. If they are marked, they'll never pass the ball to either 7 or 11, because when you

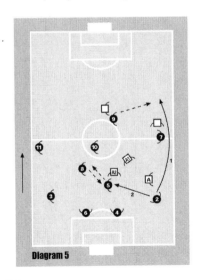

Diagram 5

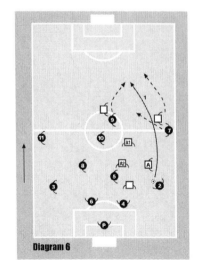

Diagram 6

are marked you should pass the ball to the marked player farthest away.

The halfbacks could also look for the central forward...

Of course, but we serve 9 with a straight ball at his feet. It's more difficult to have 9 on the outside and 10 on the inside when the halfbacks are in possession. This is more doable when the backs are in possession. If 9 receives, he can:

▸ turn around to shoot;
▸ get support from 10 who is coming in and can also serve wings 7 and 11 **(diagram 7)**;

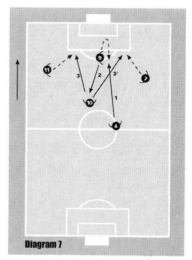

Diagram 7

On the other hand, if 9 doesn't see 10, he can be backed up by a midfield player or a wing. Then 10 will follow **(diagram 8)**.

Also the player positioned in the final third (10) can receive and then 9 cuts behind or in front of the defender, depending on the marking. As a last option 9 can receive in deep and accelerate for:

▸ a shot or a cross, if he can see the goal **(diagram 9)**;
▸ covering the ball and serving 7 or 11, if he can't see the goal **(diagram 10)**.

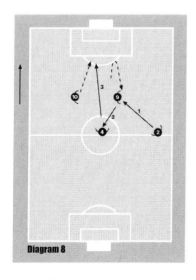

Diagram 8

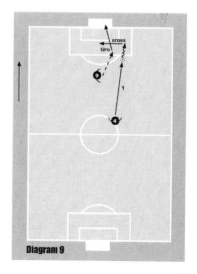

Diagram 9

57

What if the halfbacks have to keep the ball moving?

After passing the ball between 5 and 8 (**diagram 11**), 11 can either receive wide, if the defender closes him down, or he can receive inside, if the defender stays wide. The back comes into the space that was created.

How can you defend - and it could happen - with only 6 players plus the goalkeeper?

I tell you right now that I don't think it's possible to defend with 6 players only. It's possible with 7 or 8 players, but not with 6. When defending with 6 players (4 defenders and 2 central half-

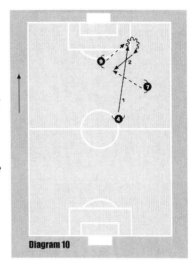

Diagram 10

backs), the midfield players can only play to stop the opponents from playing deep penetrating balls for the forwards. There are two major issues:

▸ for the opponents it's too easy to find their outer players free (A and A1) since - with B or B1 in possession - 2 and 3 must stay in a defensive position, meaning they must be far from A and A1 (**diagram 12**);

▸ if 2 and 3 would be marking A and A1 a bit more - not playing in a defensive position as much and in case of a pass from B to C1 -

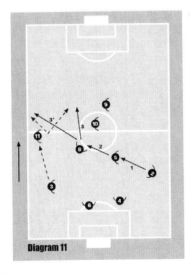

Diagram 11

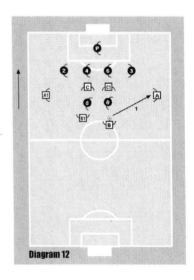

Diagram 12

it would be possible to create a dangerous 1 v 1 situation between 6 and C1, since 3 is not covering (he is oriented towards A to make the reception more difficult) and 4 is must both cover and mark.

Now, how do you see the future of soccer...?

The top athletes will only train for tactics. We won't have fitness training anymore. Each athlete (it's happening already) will have his personal fitness trainer.

In the morning the player will train with the team and in the afternoon the personal trainer will supplement the tactical and technical work of the coach. For example, if in the morning you work out to train your strength, in the afternoon you will have to focus on speed and so on. This will be very important because it's impossible to have an athletic preparation program valid both for the team and the single player. Each athlete is different and each role is different.

What about the tactical aspects?

On the tactical level we need to find a mix between the organization of the ball movement (always studied and stopped by the goalkeeper) and the individual qualities. I think it is necessary to move back and create

A single voice

Everything and anything has been said about Arrigo Sacchi. For sure we can say that Sacchi has totally changed the way of playing soccer, but he didn't create soccer, as somebody (not him though) said. Certainly it's a great accomplishment to go from second category to Milan and then to the National Team, especially in such an up-tight and close environment as Italian soccer.

What formation....

Hold on...I want to stop you right away. I don't think that formations matter...

Well, this is a good way to start....

Don't misunderstand me. What I mean is that the team should not be influenced by the formation. Unfortunately in Italy...

Unfortunately what...

In Italy we play soccer in a very conservative way: totally in the back. For two reasons: a social one (this is what Italians prefer) and a sports one. We lack the culture of working hard and when you don't work hard it's easier to play in defense rather than in attack.

Then the formation is not so important?

What's important is the interpretation of the formation. I'll give you an example: when I was with Milan we were attacking with at least 5 players who were carefully maneuvering rather than passing long. I always wanted a player to act as a filter between the attackers and the defenders. Most of the time the defense was classic (1 v 1), without trying to be in situation of numerical superiority. On the other hand, since we were often attacking and in numerical inferiority, it was necessary to use the offside trap a lot.

Your formation was the....

Don't say any number. Our true formation was movement, a movement referring to the ball, to the opponents and to the field. We were trying to be leaders and we were working hard.

I remember the question you were asked in England...

Yes. I was invited to Manchester by the English Federation and the question was: "How did you make the Italians run forward and not backward?". I told them that by making the players work hard I was giving them the necessary confidence to develop our game.

The main aspects of that game are:

▸ numerical superiority in the ball area during the offensive stage;
▸ to remain very short, because if you stay closer to each other, everyone can play both in attack and defense.

But abroad...

Once Van Basten told me: "Mister, you don't work to win, but to convince!". In Holland and England they have the culture of working and losing that we miss in Italy, and without it you cannot attack.

But who's responsible for the Italian situation?

First of all the audience and the mass-media, who want you to win no matter how. Violence and deception are allowed. Abroad there isn't this kind of culture; you work hard during the week to offer a beautiful game on Sunday. For instance, I remember once a match with Juventus and Milan; after 15 minutes Juventus hit the goal and basically the match ended then. And for the audience it was just fine. The very next day it was the semifinal of Champions League and for Barcelona a tie would have been enough to pass. After only 5 minutes that the Spanish team had possession, the audience started to complain.

To be more specific, how did you organize your game during the offensive and the defensive stage?

I was mixing the global and the analytical methods. It was a very simple method. I was going from a complicated level to a very simple one. But with all my teams I always tried to maintain the positive characteristics of Italian Soccer. For instance, counterattack or the great attention for the defense, etc. I also had great attention for the technical training, both analytical and the one applied to the various exercises.

You spoke about a culture of working hard, but today there isn't much time to train, especially for the big teams that are so busy...

I propose a total turnover and I'll tell you why. When I was with Milan, if after one week I wasn't using tactical exercises, players such as Ancelotti, Baresi or Donadoni would come up to me asking for it, because they did not want to lose their game sensibility. Today the Champions League has more matches, but still sometimes not all the matches are fundamental. For us it was different, we had first and second leg matches and we could not make mistakes. Today there can be a period of fifteen days without matches during the week, and then you must work out. Having two teams gives me the chance of training my players always. In other words, the team that does not play on Sunday has to train and vice-versa.

There are other championships and the foreign players are committed to their national teams as well....

This is a problem that the owners created by themselves. Buying foreign players is allowed, but it's not mandatory. Atalanta, for instance, has only one foreign player. Only if you play hard, can you play well. During the 1999-2000 season the work was done by Verona, Atalanta and Udinese. These are all teams that consider the work done during the week as very important.

What does Arrigo Sacchi think about the future of Italian soccer?

I think we have to work harder and better. But I think we are going in the wrong direction, because we don't work during the week. The technicians are becoming more and more like managers. They are not teaching anything anymore. The team leadership belongs to the players and this means the end of soccer. In fact the economical advantage is huge and it makes the team richer, but then we miss a very important element to keep the players united, and that is the game. We are used to buying great players for incredible amounts of money, but then we forget to see if they fit with the rest of the team and if they are really useful. The leadership should go back to the coach (to his ideas and work). There are too many managers and not enough teachers. This is not good for soccer in general and especially for the technicians.

We want to remind you that this is what we propose as a structure in order to create something on your own...

4.1 4:4:2 Back player in overlapping situation (diagram 57)

The defenders pass the ball to one another and always receive after a feint. The left back player (3) passes to 8 (who has moved into a wider position) and overlaps. Now 8 can play on the forward 11 or on the mid-field player 10, who are closing the triangle so that 3 can cross. On the cross they will meet 9 and 7 (the opposing external midfield player), with 5 (the opposing central midfield player) close to the edge of the area. All this has to be repeated on the left and on the right side.
One variable of this exercise comes from the fact that, having received the ball once, 8 cannot play it directly ahead because he is attacked very tightly. At this point 8 will receive support from 10, who will serve 3 deep (diagram 57b)

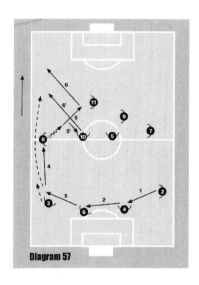

Diagram 57

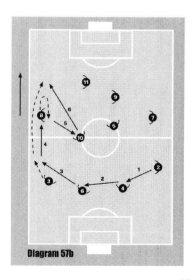

Diagram 57b

4.2 Midfield player inside and back outside (diagram 58)

When the ball is coming on 6, 8 moves wide on the line as well as 3; when 6 can "see", 8 cuts in and 3 moves into the free space.
If 8 receives: he can create a triangle with the closest forward or he can shoot, serving the diagonal movement of the other forward with the insertion of a central midfield player into the free space. Or he can play the ball deep if the other two forwards criss-cross each other.
If 3 receives: he creates a triangle with 8 to be able to cross, or 8 moves on 3 to criss-cross with him.

4.3 When the central midfield player is shooting (diagram 59)

When the right back 2 is in possession, the lateral midfield player 7 moves deep and the closest forward approaches and receives. Then 2 moves back on the central midfield player 5, 9 cuts in and 10 (the other central midfield player) moves into the free space. Then 5 can pass to 9 or to 10.

4.4 Deep movement of the forward (diagram 60)

10 serves 8 and the forward moves closer, because 8 has an opponent right in front. 8 creates a triangle with the nearest forward as the other gets ready to cut.

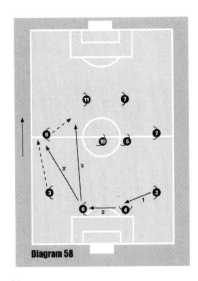

Diagram 58

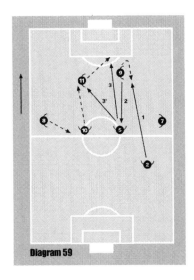

Diagram 59

4.5 Exchange of position between a central midfield player and an outer midfield player (diagram 61)

7 (the right outside midfield player) is in possession and serves 5 from behind; 10 (another central midfield player) moves forward, but in order to free himself from the marking he exchanges position with 8 (left outside midfield player).

4.6 Exchange of position between the forward and the outer midfield player (diagram 62)

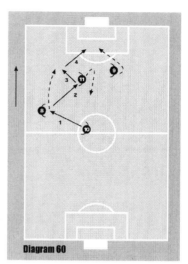

Diagram 60

With the left back (3) in possession, 8 and the nearest forward (11) are both marked and exchange position to be able to receive the ball and allow 3 to:

▶ serve 8 cutting in;
▶ serve 11 cutting out.

4.7 Movement of the outer pairs

In a 4:4:2 situation the movement of the pairs on the outer spaces is very important. The pairs are composed by the back and the outer midfield

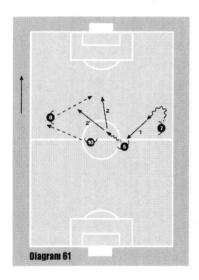

Diagram 61

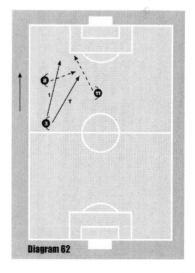

Diagram 62

player. When a central defender - who's able to see and play deep up-field - is in possession, it could happen that:

▶ one of the two players moves in depth as the other one moves forward;

▶ one of the two players moves out as the other one moves in.

Or it could happen - for instance - that the back player moves in deep and wide, and the outer midfield player cuts toward the goal. On the other hand, what it could happen is that the back moves ahead cutting toward the goal. In this case the outer midfield player would stop and broaden his position.

4.8 4:3:3 When the backs come out from behind (diagram 63)

The central defender (4), after a feint, receives the ball from the goal-keeper. He turns around and when he's able to pass, the back 2 moves in deep and the midfield player 8 moves closer.

If serving:

▶ 2 can end the exercise;

▶ 8 turns around and serves 2 who's again attacking in depth, with the wing (7) moving to the center to create more space.

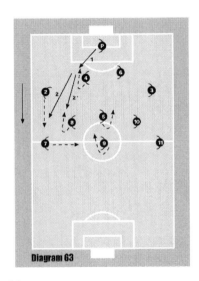

Diagram 63

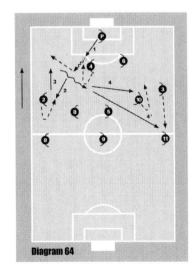

Diagram 64

4.9 When the backs come out from behind, but with switching of play (diagram 64)

Now 2 tries to dribble out, but he's closed and has to pass to 4. If it's possible, 4 turns and dribbles inside towards 3, deep on the opposite side as 10 approaches. If 4 is challenged, he gets support from 6 (behind him).

4.10 When the central halfback comes out (diagram 65)

The central halfback 5 receives the ball from 4 after a feint. After turning around, 5 serves 10, who is cutting in trying to receive the ball behind the opposing midfield players. 3 is covering the new space that was created and the wing 11 creates space by moving inward.
A variable comes from a situation where 5 cannot turn around. In this case 10 will give support receiving the ball from 5. Later on 10 will choose to pass to 3 or to the cutting 11.

4.11 How to bypass the pressure with a penetrating pass to the central forward (diagram 66)

If we are closed near the ball, we have to play a long ball forward to find a way out. In diagram 66 you see that 2 - after playing trying to dribble up-field and being closed down - turns and passes to 4.
With a long ball as his only option, 4 passes to the center forward (9),

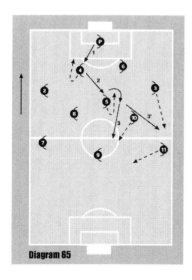

Diagram 65

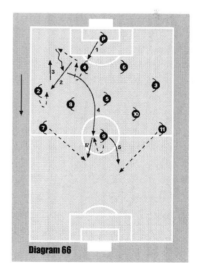

Diagram 66

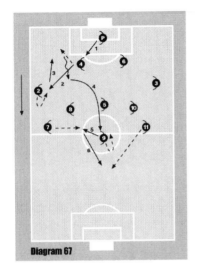

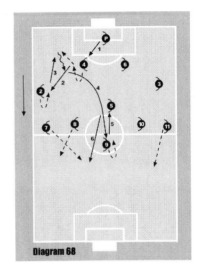

Diagram 67   Diagram 68

who has unmarked himself by faking a long run. If during the shot the two wings (7 and 11) have moved deep behind 9, the player in possession tries to extend the trajectory of the ball and serves the two wings. Vice versa - in **diagram 67** - the two wings did not move deep; in this situation we have two choices:

▸   if the midfield players are far from 9, 9 is supported by the wing facing him and the team has enough time to move up-field; the other wing 11 cuts in and 10 or 3 move into the free space that has been created;

▸   if the midfield players are close, they receive the ball and then they serve the wings (7 and 11) cutting in (**diagram 68**), with 8 or 10 moving into the free spaces.

4.12 How to bypass the pressure with a deep pass to the central for-ward (diagram 69)

The procedures are the same as in the previous exercises. The only difference is that 9 receives after penetrating and moving deep up-field. Here the wing on the same side (in diagram 69 it's player 7) brings immediate support to 9, as the other wing 11 is ready to mark in depth. We must say that since it's a deep pass, it's hard for the team to be next to 9 while he's receiving.
More than ever it's necessary to place the wings following the principle that "one gives support and the other moves in depth". Two are the goals we would like to achieve:

Diagram 69

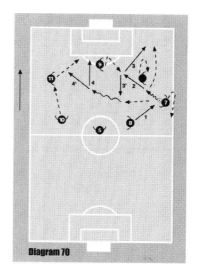

Diagram 70

> we want to maintain possession of the ball in order to have enough time to move up;

> we want to attack deeply when the opposing defense is in a bad position.

In a 4: 3: 3 formation it's important that the width is won by the wings, in case of actions coming from the back; the midfield players are often involved in the game after the forwards have received the ball, so they can either give support or insert into the free spaces.

Let's consider now a few "high" movements. In other words, those situations where we can shoot at goal. Our plan is to create a 2 v 1 situation on the outer players or a 2 v 2 situation up-field. If this is not possible, then we should change our game in the opposite half of the field.

4.13 Penetration of the wing and other developments (diagram 70)

The wing attacks the back from behind. The back withdraws and allows the wing to receive the ball at his feet. If the wing has enough space, he can:

> beat the opponent with a triangle together with 9 and then cross pass to 9 and 11;

> beat the opponent with a triangle together with 9 and then either serve 11 cutting in, the insertion of 10 or shoot at goal.

This movement should be done if - as we pass from 7 to 9 - the defender slides in the back preventing 7 from receiving. The advantages are:

▶ the back is subjected to a movement in the area behind him;

▶ the dynamic of this action makes 9 and his marker a block for the back who's trying to come up-field. An alternative to this is a 1 v 1 situation (**diagram 70b**):

▶ as you can see 7 beats the defender inside and serves 9 or 11 cutting in with 10. 10 moves into the free space.

▶ or 7 beats the defender outside and crosses (**diagram 70c**).

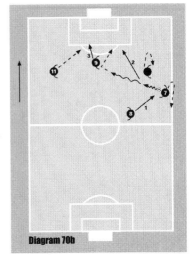

Diagram 70b

It could also happen that the ball moves toward the wing who can't turn, but can only pass to a supporter (**diagram 72**).

The action can continue with 7 starting long and with 9 starting short, serving him deeply or switching the play.

The pass is necessary also when the wing is doubled up (but it has to be done correctly, otherwise we can try an insertion between the two defenders, **diagram 73**).

Diagram 70c

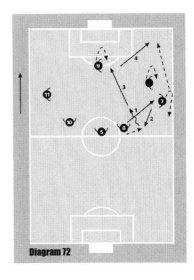

Diagram 72

4.14 Overlapping of the midfield player or of the back on the wing

Overlapping is a good way to create a 2 v 1 situation. When the wing receives the ball at his feet, he can play the ball forward and we can run deep behind him.

The overlapping may not create a local 2 v 1, but it can force the opponents into the ball area while the opposite area gets uncovered and is used for dangerous insertions.

In **diagram 74** we see that 8 - after serving 7 - overlaps so that 7 can:

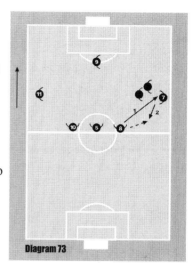

Diagram 73

▸ pass the ball to 9, who serves 8 for a cross;

▸ create a triangle inside with 9, in case 7 can't serve 8 on the side;

▸ it could also happen that 7 is closed down and can't play forward. But also in this case it's possible to overlap, if there is a third player to get support from.

In **diagram 75** we see that 8, closed by 7, cannot pass and overlap at the same time. But if 5 or 2 can give their support to 7, then 8 speeds up, receives behind 7 and cross passes.

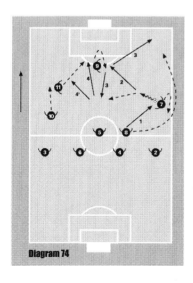

Diagram 74

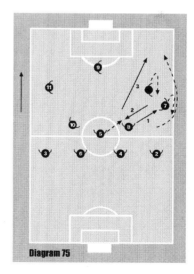

Diagram 75

This movement is called 1-2-3 from the number of passes done. But if the overlapping is done by 2, then 8 will act as the third supporting player (**diagram 76**).

4.15 Diagonal movement of the wing

When the wing is marked tightly, but the defender leaves a lot of space inside, the wing should cut toward the inner part of the field. The diagonal movement creates a space that has to be taken by another player so that the player in possession has two possibilities to pass the ball.

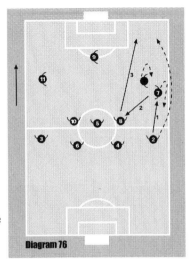

Diagram 76

In **diagram 77** we see 8 in possession, 7 cuts in and 2 moves into the free space.

If 7 receives: he will try to serve 9 and 11 cutting in, with 10 into the free space. Or he will just shoot.

If 2 receives: he can create a triangle with 7 and proceed with a cross. Or it could be 7 cutting in front and then making the cross pass.

In **diagram 78** instead, we see the situation where 2 is in possession. 8 will take the free space created by 7 cutting in. The developments are the

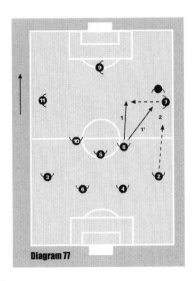

Diagram 77

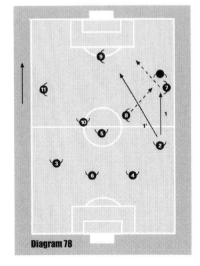

Diagram 78

72

same, the only variable is that - if in possession - 8 has the same options as 2 before.

4.16 Penetrating movements of the central forward

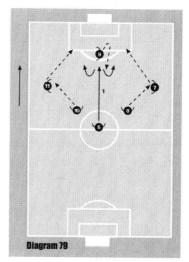

In this case there are two different situations:

▸ the defender is pressing and can't turn around;
▸ the defender is not pressing and is able to turn around.

Diagram 79

In the first case the attacker is able to turn around and serve the wings (7 and 11) cutting in, with the midfield players (8 and 10) into the free spaces **(diagram 79)**. It could also happen that the movement becomes faster because - if on the pass from 5 to 9 - 7 or 11 enter into the space (but 9 is able to serve them) and the speed of the action increases. Then 7 or 11 will serve the other wing and shoot **(diagram 80)**. The case is different if 9 (under pressure) can only pass to the back.

In **diagram 81** we see that 9 receives from 8 and can only pass back to 5. Then he'll be in charge of serving the wings and the midfield players on the side cutting in.

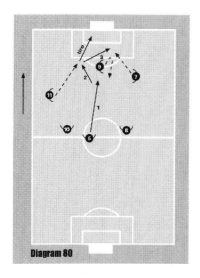

Diagram 80

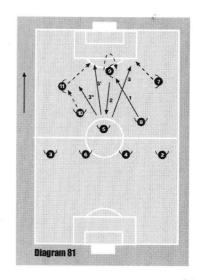

Diagram 81

73

The show must go on

To summarize Renzo Ulivieri's career is not easy. It's an adventure begun in Empoli in Serie C in the 1970's and with many achievements. In 1982 he moved up to Serie A with Sampdoria. He also passed from C to B with Modena and Vicenza . But his masterpiece was done with Bologna: in 1994 he took the team from Serie C1 to Serie A. He's now coaching an important team, Parma.

Where does the need for 3:4:2:1 come from? (diagram 1)
It comes from the fact that I wanted to oppose the dominant 4:4:2. With this formation I was troubling them because I was attacking the players in the middle. In fact the two makeshift strikers, converging behind the vertex, were forcing the two backs to come in to control, then they were attacking with the two external midfield players. The advantage decreases against a three man defense always playing with a 1 v 1. But the three men in defense suffer against three forwards laid out with two wide wings and a central wing.

Keep in mind that each formation originates from the attackers' characteristics, and the rest follows.

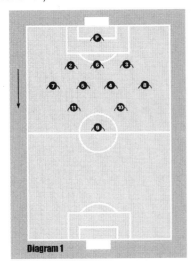

Diagram 1

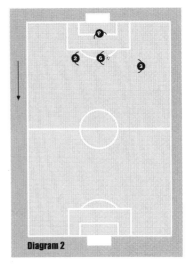

Diagram 2

What are the limitations of this formation?
The overuse of the external midfield players, who have to work very hard. They have a big part of the field to cover, but they also have to be good in the offensive stage, since they often must move forward. And as we said, we could have some problems against the three wide forwards.

How do you organize the possession of the ball?
There are two ways to build the action: the short way with the ball on the ground and the high way with a forward. In Bologna we had Kennet Andersson. When we were in a good condition we were able to alternate the two ways; when we were too lazy, we were playing even ten long balls one after the other and - in this way - we were very predictable. When the three defenders were dribbling from behind, the concept was to have a wide supporter and two supporters toward the inside for the whole width of the penalty area **(diagram 2)**. Sometimes the central one of the three players - in case one of the two central midfield players cuts in deep - would move up to the center into the free space to create a condition of numerical superiority **(diagram 3)**. The main concept driving us was the search for depth, otherwise we would play wide and toward the inside; but if we were marked by the central midfield players, we were playing externally on the forwards. One of the makeshift strikers was coming under the forward depending on where he was going **(diagram 4 and 5)**.

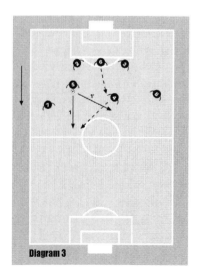

Diagram 3

Diagram 4

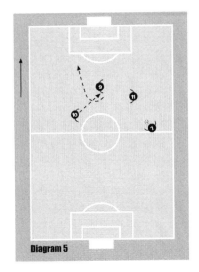

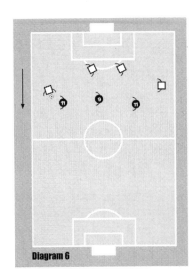

Diagram 5

Diagram 6

What if it wasn't possible to build the action in the short way?
If we were under pressure, we would often pass to the central player who
was overlapping the forward placed in front; but if we were in the other
half of the field, the central player could also play deep. Of course in this
situation 9 would often come forward to stay close to the team and prevent his teammates from playing long passes, which are hard to control.

What were your basic principles during the defensive stage?
If the opponents were playing with three defenders, we would face them
with a 3 v 3, with two makeshift strikers and one forward. The case was
different if we were playing against a defense with 4 men. On a lateral
ball it was easy because 11 or 10 were attacking the opposing back and 9
- together with the other makeshift striker - would move on the nearest
opposing supporters, freeing the opposing back (**diagram 6**). Another
situation was with the ball in the center and 9 in a 1 v 2 . As long as the
two opposing central defenders exchange passes, 9 can ''dance'' between
the two of them. When one of the two moves toward a back, then we
start pressing (**diagram 7**). Another situation is the one where the opposing central defender tries to move in deep; in this case the midfield players will mark him.

How many players were you taking behind the ball line?
Most of the time our defense had seven players plus one of the two
makeshift strikers (the one opposing the ball and penetrating together
with the midfield players, **diagram 8**). The two outside midfield players,
from the final third down, were either playing as a fourth defender or
staying in midfield.

76

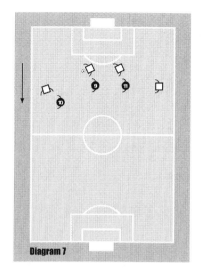

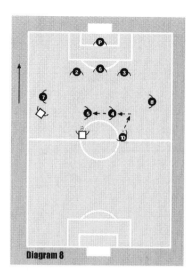

Diagram 7   Diagram 8

What if you were playing against one or three forwards?

In this case it was important to have a very good right central player (2) so that he could play both centrally and on the outside, or even move forward as a midfield player. In such a case I would make this player move wider, while the others were moving toward the midfield. Such a player should be very good and tactically mature. In Bologna I had Paramatti who had all these skills.

Let's talk about the work on the field...

At the beginning I was starting with a global approach, both for the defensive and the offensive stage. First I would lay out the teams 11 v11, then I would analyze the positions according to these options:

▸ without opponents;
▸ with passive opponents and with active opponents.

During the season I would stop for one week to allow the players to relax, but then they would come to me on their own to ask for those exercises again.

Do you often change formation during a match?

If the team is mature tactically, it's possible. You can move from a defense with 3 or 4 players. For the offensive stage it's not that easy. The offensive stage needs subtler movements and so it's harder to change it during a game.

Do you think it's useful to change according to the opposing team?

There is a basic formation and the changes can stand for small things such as:

77

- to attack more on one side;
- to build a long or a short action;
- to cross from the final third or from the back;
- to vary the pressing;
- marking on certain players.

What should be the formation for the junior team?

I think the basic formation to teach the youth should be the 4: 3: 3 with total zone. This formation lets you propose moving roles like the wings and it's the most instructive for the kids because it "forces" each one of them to play. With this formation we will vary the roles, each player has to try (at least once!) the emotion of playing with number 10. It's also a formation with which it's easy to identify the different roles and their functions.

How do you see soccer in the future?

More open-minded. With more chances to score because we need a better show and the score does help. But the coaches are becoming more and more like managers. Even in Serie A we need more teaching. We should find the right ways (meaning different methods) because often there isn't the will to learn. But this is rare. Most of the time everybody wants to learn.

Attack...seriously!

Andrea Mandorlini is young for his age, his career and his role as a coach. After a few years as "assistant" to coaches such as Novellino, Cavasin, and Sandreani, he started to walk alone in Trieste, where he missed the promotion to Serie C1 during the play-off. His masterpiece came in the 1999-2000 season, while coaching La Spezia in C2, when he won the championship with 0 (zero) defeats . Amazing! This year, in C1, he's hoping to move up to Serie B...

Andrea, why should we lay out a 3:4:1:2?

Because if you have a player positioned in the final third like Zidane, it is better to use him. I'm talking about a player very good at receiving from the forwards, good at attacking the free spaces or at winning possession between the midfield and the opposing defense.

And of course he has to be technically good, able to attack and with initiative.

With this formation what advantages do you think you will have during the offensive stage?

I gain width with the two outside midfield players and depth with the three forwards **(diagram 1)**; in case of a defense with 4 opponents the central players are in a 1 v 1 situation. If the game is open, I ask the other forwards to play deep in order to move away from the line and allow the final third player to receive the ball. But if the game is closed, I try to move beside the forwards. With three tight forwards (two plus one) nobody accepts the 1 v 1; that is why the backs get involved and move behind the outside midfield players. In this way I gain numerical superiority in midfield and I look for an outside 1 v 1 situation with the midfield players.

Diagram 1

And on a defensive level?
I still have numerical superiority in the center, but if the opponents also have three forwards, I maintain a 3 v 3.
During the defensive stage there is no final third player, he moves next to the forwards and supports the defense.

What do you think should be the requirements for the goalkeepers and the three defenders?
I want the goalkeeper to be keen, able to read the situation and communicate with the team. He has to be good at playing with his feet because we often pass the ball to him; he should also be able to kick the ball out. For the defenders, ability is not a fundamental quality, they have to be very good at defending and reading each situation. I often make them practice with "high" situation (from our goal line) as it happens normally on Sunday.

Let's talk about the outside midfield players....
I could say that I have a staff of 5 players for 2 roles. They have to be able to run and be very good in the offensive stage. They must be able to close the field with a cross in the opposite half and win 1 v 1 situations with:

▸ ability;
▸ strength;
▸ 1-2 (one-two).

The defensive stage of the midfield players - on the other hand - depends on the three forwards because, if they don't make a sacrifice and filter, the midfield players cannot move up.

And the central midfield players?
Fundamental! My defensive "castle" is made by the central midfield players and the three defenders; they run vertically and laterally together. One has to be good at playing and the other at winning possession of the ball. I would like to make clear that with a long ball on the forwards, it's up to these players to receive from behind and so it's up to the outside midfield players to close the field because they are very close to the area of reception.

Finally, what about the forwards?
One has to be good at heading and pressing, the other two must be fast, good in 1 v 1 and technically capable. The player positioned in the final third must be able to play "important" balls. So my principle for the forwards is:

▸ open game: play long;
▸ closed game: come forward.

How do you organize your work on the field?

On a defensive level I start right from the basics: 1 v1 , 1 v 2, 1 v 2 with the goalkeeper, 2 v 2, 3 v 2, 3 v 3, etc.. I add the two halfbacks to the defense and then the outside midfield players. Then I make my three defenders play against three tight forwards, three wide forwards, two forwards plus the final third player. On the offensive level I start with or without passive opponents. I try to look at the different situations, the mind level in Serie C is different from Serie A.

We know sometimes you dream (it actually happened a few times) of playing with...

You can say it, two defenders, one halfback in front, four midfield players, three forwards.

In other words you are for attacking...

Listen, I had this kind of mentality also when I was a player and I had coaches who taught me more about managing the group rather than about teaching. What helped me a lot though, was working as an assistant coach.

How do you see the future of soccer?

We will have to be able to better "read" the ball and, consequently, the situations. And even if it seems that the counterattack is the kind of soccer that pays the dues more, I believe in a truly offensive soccer. A kind of soccer where you can attack with at least 5 or 6 players and not with one or 2 only; a kind of soccer where we try to bring numerical superiority and do it well.

The problem of the defense with 3 players is a little different from the defense with 4 players. We should keep in mind that nobody defends with only 3 or 4 players. What is really important is how many elements I take behind the ball line when in possession. For some other aspects you can go back to chapter 1, where we have covered these topics very well.

5.1 To rationally fill the space

The first issue that we must face is the rational distribution of the defenders so that the spaces near the ball are well covered without emptying the ones that are further down.

In **diagram 82** we see B passing to C and the 3 defenders "sliding" towards the new player in possession, while 2 (defender facing the ball) pays attention not to go beyond the far post.

Afterwards C will pass the ball to B **(diagram 83)** and the defense will move to the center. The exercise can continue with the 3 players A, B and C dribbling and the defense trained to move accordingly. A variable of the exercise sees the ball dribbled (the coach or another player is in possession) either to the right, to the left, to the center, to the back or to the front.

In this case we not only must adapt as we did in the previous situation, but we also have to move forward or back (tactical defensive run) depending on where the ball is going **(diagram 84)**.

Very important: we must keep a standard distance of 20 yards from the ball, calculated on the reaction time of the defenders in case the goalkeeper passes deep up- field. In **diagram 85** we see that the midfield has been added to the

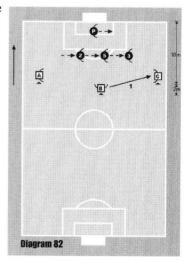

Diagram 82

defensive position and the exercise is done with the dribbling of A, B and C; in this case the midfield has 4 players, but it's clear that each coach will lay out the position according to the formation he's using. The next step **(diagram 86)** will be to insert the defense and complete the team with three forwards.
The whole thing has to be repeated with the player in possession moving around.

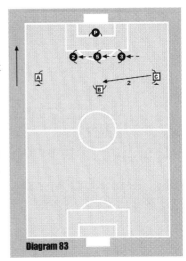

Diagram 83

5.2 Coming out and covering of the opposing player in possession

Now, to the cover of the spaces, we will add a defender coming out on the opposing player in possession and the covering movements of the other two players; as you can see in **diagram 87**, with a lateral ball - as 3 comes out on the player in possession C - 5 covers the player in possession, while 2 is in line with 5. In **diagram 88** we present a central situation where 5 comes out closing on the player in possession (B) and 2 and 3 guarantee the cover creating a triangle. The exercise is about pointing out the player A, B or C as the one in possession; the situation practices closing and covering.
This happens with the dribbling of the 3 players A, B and C who are

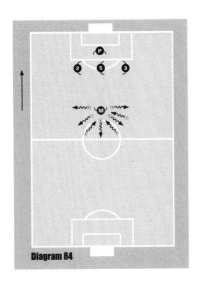

Diagram 84

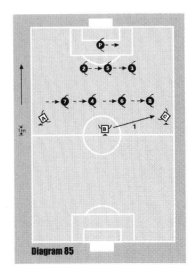

Diagram 85

passing the ball at the sound of the coach's whistle.

We want to add a forward on the defensive line (D) and then two forwards (D and E), who will have to be marked maintaining the appropriate blocking and covering **(diagram 89 and 90)**. Following the methodology we will add the midfield position. Now we are going to have fun!

When we consider the defense with three players, the capacity of the outside midfield players to read the ball position is fundamental; in fact many coaches define these as balance players. In **diagram 91** (always with the midfield with 4 players) we see the position coming out on a

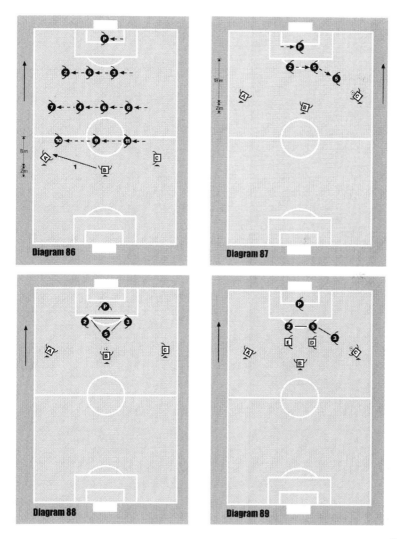

Diagram 86

Diagram 87

Diagram 88

Diagram 89

lateral ball and we see that the problem results from the outlined area not being covered by any defenders.

If the opposing players are not present, there is no problem. But what happens if there are opposing players? We would have two situations:

▸ open ball **(diagram 92)**: the opposing player in possession sees our goal and he can play deep. In this case 8 will have to play more or less on the defensive line depending on the position of the opponent G;

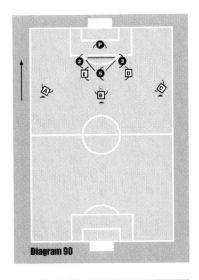

Diagram 90

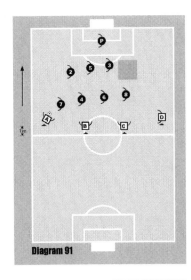

Diagram 91

Diagram 92

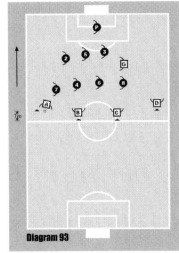

Diagram 93

►   closed ball **(diagram 93)**: the opposing player in possession can not see our goal or he sees it but cannot play deep. In this case 8 will play moving towards the ball but without leaving the mid field line.

This is a fundamental principle for an effective defensive stage. If this doesn't happen, the situation would be quite risky for our position in the back during fast game changes. Our position would be forced to maintain a "long" line, widening the space between the three defenders.

During his interview, Marcello Lippi offered the variable of the insertion of the central halfback between the defenders to put together the position in case of unbalance.

In **diagram 94** we see the central closing of the midfield players, who must be careful to close the space approaching one another. The methodology is always the same:

►   the coach points out a player (supposedly the one in possession);
►   players A, B, C and D pass the ball to one another at the sound of the coach's whistle;
►   players A, B, C and D pass the ball to one another freely;
►   we add two forwards on the defensive line and 1 or 2 players on the midfield line.

We end with the evaluation of the situation of the player in possession. If he can see, the defenders will slowly mark the forwards on the line and the midfield players will cover more closely the man who came out on

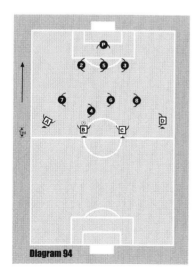

Diagram 94

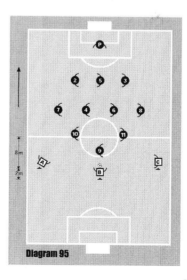

Diagram 95

the player in possession. If he cannot see, the defenders will mark the forwards more and the midfield players will be more aggressive. Then we must add the fact that the outside midfield players facing the ball (with a lateral ball) should evaluate - depending on the ball position and on the presence or not of an opponent - if they have to play as a fourth defender or not.

Then we add the forwards and we repeat the exercise (**diagram 95**).

5.3 Passing the marking duties from one defender to the next

The reader can easily understand the methodology by looking at the paragraph where we talk about the defense with 4 players. Of course you have to adapt the principles to only 3 players and add the positions and the opponents progressively (see paragraph 1.2).

5.4 To neutralize penetrating runs, triangular passing, overlapping, shots and headers, penetrating passes, back passes and marking against crosses

Also in this case we ask you to look at the paragraphs on the defense with 4 players. Of course you must adapt the principles to the new disposition with 3 players (see paragraphs 1.3 to 1.8 and 1.11).

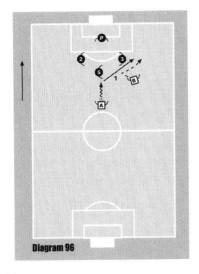

Diagram 96

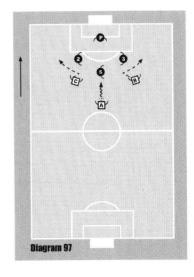

Diagram 97

5.5 Issues with 3 v 2, 3 v 3 and 3 v 4

We would like to analyze a few issues in the defense with 3 players:
Situation with 3 v 2: in **diagram 96** the player in possession dribbles
centrally toward 5, 2 and 3 cover, as B gives support to A: if B moves
toward 3, who's marking him, we can have two situations:

▸ if 3 covers it too tightly, B can receive the ball since he's free;
▸ 3 must find a position where he can mark and cover at the same
time, and in case the player in possession A doesn't serve B, or
he cannot see B anymore, A must go back to cover.

Situation with 3 v 3: in **diagram 97** we see that the previous situation
can take place also with two opposing supporters (B/C) who try to broad-
en the defenders 2 and 3 on the cover. This would allow an easier 1 v 1
for A with 5. In this case we would have:

▸ 2 is behaving as 3 did previously, but with one variable, the
defender marking the opponent in the visual field of the player
in possession will tend to mark more, while the other will tend
to cover more.

In **diagram 98** A sees B and 3 is marking him very closely, while 2
moves closer to 5 to cover.
Situation 3 v 4: the principle says that in case of numerical inferiority
you have to play for time and move back to:

▸ receive support from a teammate;
▸ defend in small space and receive support from the goalkeeper if

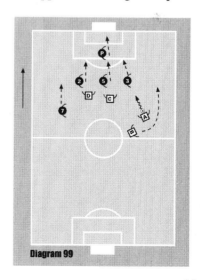

Diagram 98

Diagram 99

there aren't other teammates taking their position.

In **diagram 99** we see that the local 2 v 1 is absorbed by 7 retaking his position from the defensive line; in this way we restore a situation of numerical equality of 4 v 4. In **diagram 100** we have a central situation (always with numerical inferiority) where A serves B, who's moving deep up-field for the insertion of C. 2 and 3 are covering 5 and marking D and E at the same time.

Now 3 has the problem of having two players to mark. Remember the principle that says when there are two oppo-

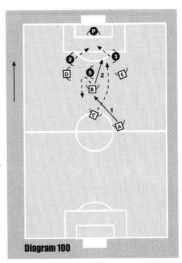

Diagram 100

nents present in your area, you must control the opponent near the goal. In this case 3 moves together with C towards the goal, leaving E more free. Also 2 comes in, but it's not so fundamental.

5.6 Doubling the marking

In case of defense with 3 men and 4 midfield players facing them we can see the following mechanisms taking place: the coach **(diagram 101)** sends the ball to the side and the defense slides with 2 coming out on the ball and 7 doubling; on the other side we have the same action between 3

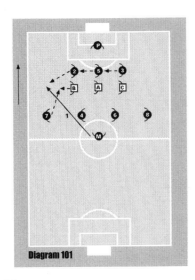

Diagram 101

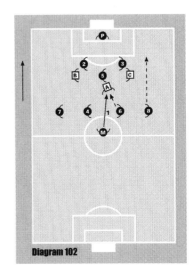

Diagram 102

and 8.

With a central ball **(diagram 102)** we have the coach passing the ball to A with 5 closing him and 2 and 3 covering: If necessary, 8 retakes his position and 6 doubles up. On the other side **(diagram 103)** 2 closes down on B, with 4 doubling while 7 retakes his place into a position with 4 players. The situation is different if we have a midfield with 5 players; on a lateral ball from the coach, 2 and 7 double, while on the other side we have 3 and 11 **(diagram 104)**.

In case 7 and 11 are not placed to double the marking - either because

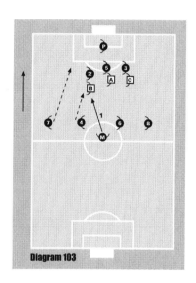

Diagram 103

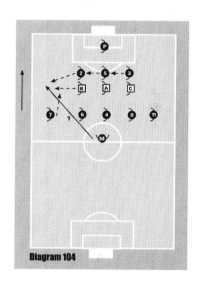

Diagram 104

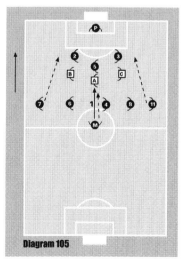

Diagram 105

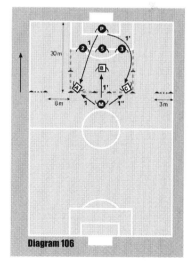

Diagram 106

91

they are too far or too late - the doubling is guaranteed by 6 on 2 and by 8 on 3.

With a central ball on A, 5 is closing down, 4 is doubling, 2 and 3 are covering and 11 is coming in to balance the position. **(diagram 105)**.

5.7 A few training exercises

3 v 3 plus the goalkeeper with offside trap and counterattack **(diagram 106)**:

▶ the coach passes to A, B or C who must score a goal;

▶ the defenders, if in possession, have to spread between the lateral goals;

Variable: you should repeat this with the defensive line placed right before the midfield line.

9 v 7 plus the goalkeeper **(diagram 107)**:

▶ the 9 attackers have to score in the big goal defended by the goalkeeper;

▶ the 7 defenders (positioned as a 3:4) must counterattack on the three small goals placed on the midfield line. You can also use the 9 players of the attacking team, using a formation that you think your opponents will use in the next match.

Variable: in case of a defensive 3:5:2 formation, the situation will be 10 v 8 (positioned as a 3:5) plus the goalkeeper as in **diagram 108**.

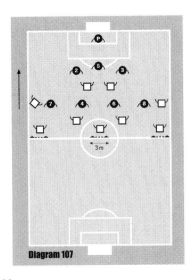

Diagram 107

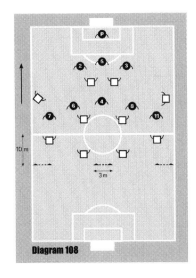

Diagram 108

Call them specialists

Ezio Glerean's career began as coach and player in 1988 in Marostica in second category. From there he won two promotions and moved to Caerano; then he took off flying. Three years in San Dona, then he moved up to C2. Now he's in Cittadella, where after two promotions he took the team to Serie B.

Where does this 3:3:4 come from?

To win you must be good in attack, the more attackers you have the better. It's a matter of making these players participate in the defensive stage without spoiling their qualities. In fact everybody knows that, in general, those who have quality don't have much quantity.

How do you obtain all this?

In my 3:3:4 (**diagram 1**) the 4 attackers retake their position centrally and not externally.

Actually we defend with three players plus 3 midfield players, to whom we add the attackers. In other words we have 6 players defending and 4 attacking.

How do you close on the defensive level, centrally or laterally?

It all depends on the distance between the positions and on the speed of the opposing offensive action. If there is no time, on the pass between A and B the midfield player comes out, otherwise the defender comes out and the action slides as in **diagram 2**.

If there is no 2 v 2, the midfield player 8 moves on to double, otherwise he slides inside. On a central ball, if the opponents have two wide forwards and one central forward, we cover the center (**diagram 4**) and we don't worry about

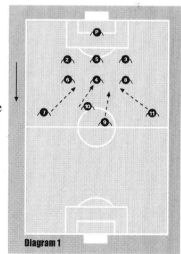

Diagram 1

the two wide players.

With this offensive formation of the attackers you can represent these two situations based on the search for a 1-2 between A and B:

▸   8 doesn't follow, the central 5 absorbs the insertion of A and 8 moves in to cover **(diagram 5)**;

▸   if 8 follows, nothing happens **(diagram 6)**.

In the search for an external 2 v 1:

▸   if the midfield player 8 has enough time, he'll close on the leader and defender 3 will "absorb" the insertion **(diagram 7)**;

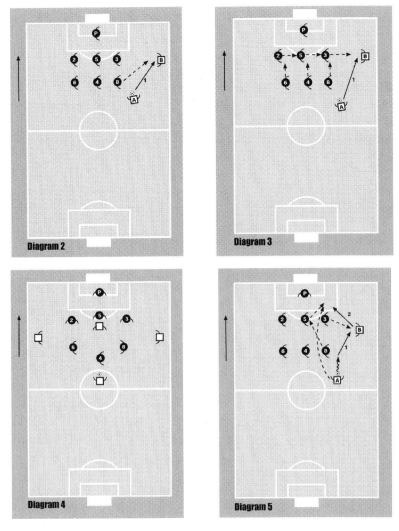

Diagram 2

Diagram 3

Diagram 4

Diagram 5

▸   if **8** does not have enough time, it will be up to the defenders to neutralize the 2 v 1 and **8** can retake his place to balance the position again (**diagram 8**).

Diagram 6

What do you ask of your players during the defensive stage?

The idea is to defend with 6 players, but when the team is pressed against the area, the forwards also come in.

You should keep in mind that it's not always possible to double up, so I often play with the defenders in a 1 v 1 and 2 v 2 situation. I always train the defense with a 3 plus 3, trying to have the players quickly reading the ball position, the time and the distance depending on the opponents' action.

As for the methodology I start with an analytical work, then I move into an exercise with the opponents. For instance if I have 20 players, we play 6 plus the goalkeeper against 14 and I stop the action each time there is mistake.

What if you play against a team with 3 forwards?

We have 4 defenders and 2 midfield players.

Talking about the offensive stage, what are the principles that rule your maneuver?

I have 4 players who can determine how to play, they have quality. I pro-

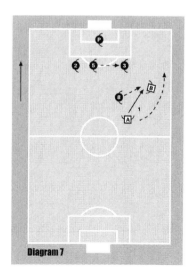

Diagram 7

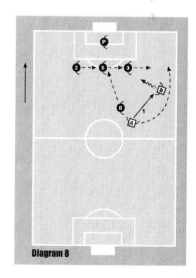

Diagram 8

pose some movements, but there is room for creativity. The 2 outside players keep their position and then they either look for the 1-2 or depth. The makeshift striker plays between the opposing midfield and defensive lines, and the central forward plays on the defenders.

A very important concept is that we never begin an action with the ball coming from behind, because we already have two lines (defense and midfield) in numerical inferiority. We always play the ball back because we have many players in front and on the header of central forward there are the makeshift strikers and two outside players.

Can you explain to us a few offensive themes?

For example with the makeshift striker in possession **(diagram 9)**, there is a Diagonal movement of the central forward and of the outside player in his visual field; the other outside player moves in. On the other hand, on the 1-2 of the outer player with the central forward **(diagram 10)** there is the diagonal movement of the makeshift striker and of the other outer player.

What are the skills that you look for in the different positions?

The defenders should be good in the 1 v 1 and at challenging the ball because often, playing with this formation, you find yourselves in individual confrontations. Without these skills what kind of defender is that? Also the defenders have a very simple duty during the offensive stage, once they have won possession of the ball, they should play short (if possible) onto the midfield players or send a long ball to the forwards. The midfield players also have (as the defenders) some mostly defensive duties. The forwards, on the other hand:

Diagram 9

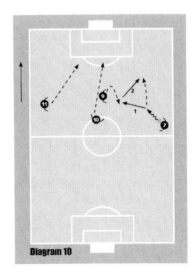

Diagram 10

96

- the outer forwards should be good in the offensive 1 v 1;
- the makeshift striker should see the game and have the skills of a second forward;
- the central forward should be strong physically.

I think this formation is good also for the youth because:
- the defenders defend;
- the midfield players act as such;
- the forwards are forwards, meaning the roles are specific.

What do you think about changing formation "while in a game"?
You must have players ready to do so. We train to defend 3 plus 3 or 4 plus 2. And this I can change anytime because I have practiced it. Any other thing is more as a back-up, like if I am 10 minutes from the end and I'm losing and I bring in a fifth attacker. In other words you can organize the team during the defensive stage, but if during the offensive stage there is no quality....

What does Ezio Glerean think about the future of soccer?
I see that when I was playing in San Dona it was all different. For example we were doing more horizontal passes and not as many vertical passes; the evolution is inside us, even keeping the same formation.
Sometimes the players do show you the way of changing, for example by interpreting the role of the central defender (the most difficult), Zanon gave a few solutions I haven't thought about. Every time we move up to the next class, people tell me: "so now we won't play"; but many times the qualities of a single player are highlighted by the play systems. 5 of the 6 defensive "specialist" players who were playing in C2 also play in B. Many players coming from the regional level can play in Serie B, sometimes it's just a matter of "use".

Order, organization, fantasy

Our series of interviews with the coaches continues with a name not as famous as the ones seen before, but still very interesting. In fact we don't believe that the ability of a coach is expressed by the class he works in. Also our man will be able to talk about a couple of topics unknown to the famous ones.

Claudio Terzulli, born in 1958, started his career in 1988 with the junior team of Rovereto, where he moved up to the first team and won the amateur championship. In 1999-2000 he moved up to C2 and now he coaches Castel San Pietro.

When did you choose the 3:4:3 ?(diagram 1)
Since the beginning of 1990 when most of the teams were either playing man-to-man or using a classic 4:4:2 by zone.
This formation would allow me to have an extra man in midfield (to close and press better) with 7 players and not 6 like with the 4:4:2. Mine is a 3:4:3 with 3 tight forwards. So I can have the wings free for the insertion of the lateral midfield players. In the back I also have the 3 v 2 to my advantage. In my half of the field the defensive line has 5 players, in the other half the defensive line has 3 players.

During the blocking stage what is the advantage of a formation with the 3 forwards laid out your way?
The advantage stands against a 4:4:2 in case the opponents place two forwards and one makeshift striker.
We try to lead the opposing game on the back player and then move to pressing; let's look at the forward far from the ball (A in **diagram 2**):

▸ if the opposing attacking center

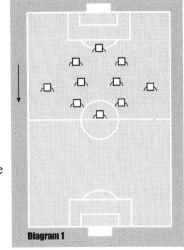

Diagram 1

half comes on the ball, he marks him to prevent him from receiving;
▶ if this doesn't happen, he moves to block the other opposing cen-   tral defender or the back (if the ball changes direction).
Closing down the attacking center half allows me to "free" one of my midfield players who can now mark the opposing makeshift striker. If there are two forwards and one makeshift striker coming against me, and the makeshift striker is in front of the two midfield players while one forward moves wide, I maintain a 3 v 3 in the back. Many coaches are afraid of numerical equality in the back, but I think it's important that if the ball is far from my goal, then I have time to take my position again. The 1 v 1 in the back is never dangerous if the forward is behind my goal. It's dangerous in the opposite case. The idea is to defend far from the goal; of course if I'm close, I have to narrow the spaces and I have to place many more defensive covers.

Why, on the other hand, do you have 3 tight forwards in the offensive stage?

Because **(diagram 3)** the two backs of the 4 : 4 : 2 were never coming out to get 11 and 7, whereas the two central were in a 2 v 1 situation against 9. This allowed 7 or 11 to receive the ball between the opposing midfield and the opposing defensive line. Or the opponents would place themselves with 3 man-markings plus a free back, losing a man in midfield. My principles in the offensive game are:
▶ to attack the spaces;
▶ to play on the side;

Diagram 2

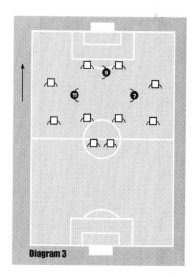

Diagram 3

- 1-2 (one-two);
- alternation of the ball on the front and on the back;
- 7 and 11 move wide: wide, straight, inside or toward; starting from this point (or from 9) we trigger the rotation of the other two players. For instance in **diagram 4**, where 7 moves in, 9 moves out and 11 moves into the space.

Let's talk about the characteristics of the goalkeeper and the 3 defenders...

The goalkeeper should be "present" physically for the inactive balls, he should know how to play with his feet and he must be able to "read" his position according to the opposing defensive line. The defenders should have a temperament, with knowledge and experience; all 3 should be good technically because often the action re-starts from the goalkeeper and they have to be able to gather and assign their position. Afterwards they must position in the field as a preventive cover, depending on where the offensive stage is happening. In fact when in possession, they only have to defend.

The midfield players...

I call the two outside midfielders "balance players", since they have great endurance and they always must find the right tactical position, meaning they either have to stay on the defensive line or on the midfield area, according to the situation.

They should be very good technically and on the offensive 1 v 1 situation. One of the two central players must have quality, in other words he should get the ball also from the defense; as the other one is more organic, meaning he should be able to press and penetrate centrally.

The 3 forwards...

The vertex should allow the other two players to play well, on the side and in depth; he should be good technically, good in the air and good in keeping possession of the ball to give the team enough time to move up. The other two attackers - they can be defined as two makeshift strikers, outside attackers or secondary forwards, must be fast and good in the offensive 1 v 1.

They should be mixed, in other words one should have the skills of a makeshift

Diagram 4

100

striker and the other should act more like a secondary forward.

How do you organize your work?

I divide the 3 stages:

- ▶   possession of the ball in my half of the field and in the other;
- ▶   non possession in any half of the field;
- ▶   positive or negative transition in my half of the field or in the other.

I start from the global level (11 v 11) and then I move to analyze each position.

How do you see soccer in 10 or 20 years?

The problem is not about past or future. Either in 2 or 100 years the job of the coach is to offer as much organization as possible to his players. Such organization should allow each player to be at his best, physically and technically.

As we have said in chapter 4, we offer a few guidelines for training the offensive stage with three defender formations. These are not rules and we remind you that the important thing is that with each plan for an offensive game you should respect the principle of ball possession explained in chapter 3.

6.1 3:5:2 "Header" of the forward (diagram 109)

2 serves the attacking center half (4) who receives after a feint. 4 is marked and passes to 2, who sends the ball to 9 (who also made a feinting maneuver). 10 and 7 move for the header of 9, with 11 giving support to 9.
Variable: this time 7 is giving support to 9, while the other forward 11 attacks the space behind 9, with 10 moving into the free space (**diagram 110**).

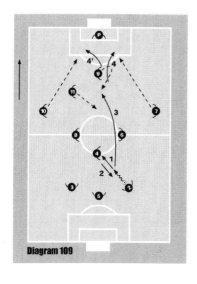

Diagram 109

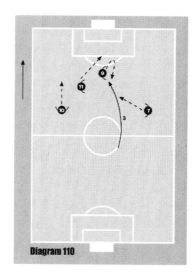

Diagram 110

6.2 Penetrating movement of the forward (diagram 111)

2 serves the forward 9 (who receives with a feint), the attacking center half 4 supports 9 who passes him the ball. The other forward 11 cuts behind 9 with the link men 10 and 7 moving deep in the field.

6.3 Attacking with a link man (diagram 112)

3 serves 6 (who receives with a feint), who is marked and passes to the attacking center half 4. 4 plays deep up-field

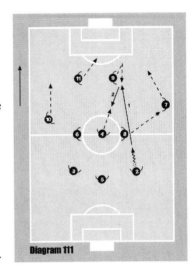

Diagram 111

and serves the link man 10, who will support: 9 cutting in, 11 moving wide and 7 moving in on the other side. All movements are aimed at putting the ball behind the opponents' defense.

Variable: 11 moves to exchange position with 10, 9 attacks the space behind 11 and 7 attacks the blind zone on the other side (**diagram 113**).

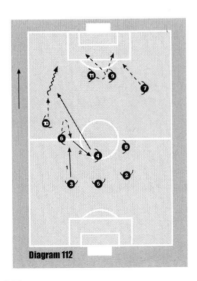

Diagram 112

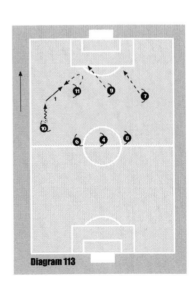

Diagram 113

104

6.4 Attacking with the link man inside (diagram 114)

The wing pair 7-8 make a maneuver with 8 going in and 7 going out, who has enough space to receive the ball. Since neither one of the two forwards moves in, 6 takes a central position under the attackers to receive.

Variable: because they are marked too much to the inside, the forwards will rotate and get open to receive with a criss-cross movement. The forward not in possession cuts in towards the goal (diagram 115).

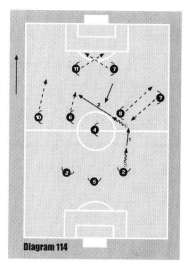

Diagram 114

6.5 Combination with three players (diagram 116)

The link man 7 moves towards 2 (who's in possession) and stays wide, 8 moves to the wing area, leaves a free space for 9 (who receives after a backward-upward feint) and passes to player 4, who serves 8 for a cross. The combination continues with the diagonal movement of the other forward (11) and with the insertion of 10.

Variable: since 9 doesn't have any support, he turns around to the inside and serves 11, who's getting ready to receive. 6 moves into the free space

Diagram 115

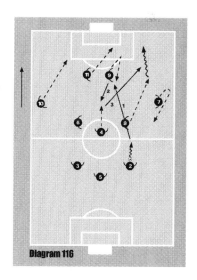

Diagram 116

105

and 8 cuts in from the right side (**dia-gram 117**).

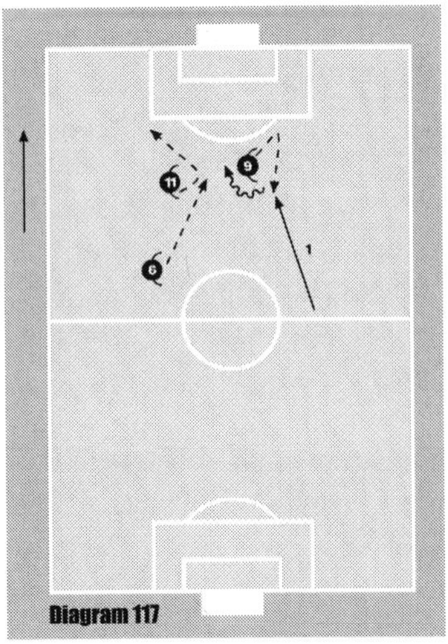

6.6 Coming out on the attacking center half (diagram 118)

The attacking center half 4 moves down (with a feint) to receive from the right central back (2). The right midfield player (8) moves wide below the link man 7 who went up-field.
Since 7 sees that the forward is not coming in, he cuts inside to receive, holding possession to wait for his teammates' insertion.

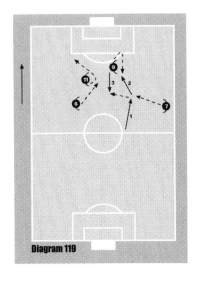

Diagram 117

Variable: the link man 7, before playing the ball toward the inside, makes a 1-2 with forward 9 to allow the exchange between the midfield player 6 and the other forward 11 (**dia-gram 119**).

6.7 Change of direction of the ball by the attacking center half (diagram 120)

The left midfield player 6 receives and - after controlling the ball - changes direction leading the ball, using the movement of 10. When the

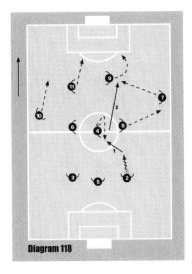

Diagram 118

Diagram 119

pass is made, 11 moves forward and the attacking central half gets ready to receive. Now the action continues with the movement of the other forward 9, who frees the space for the diagonal movement of 8 on the right.

Variable: 6 gets support from 11 (who is receiving after a feint). 11 passes on the attacking center half 4, who's serving the link man 10 on the run (**diagram 121**).

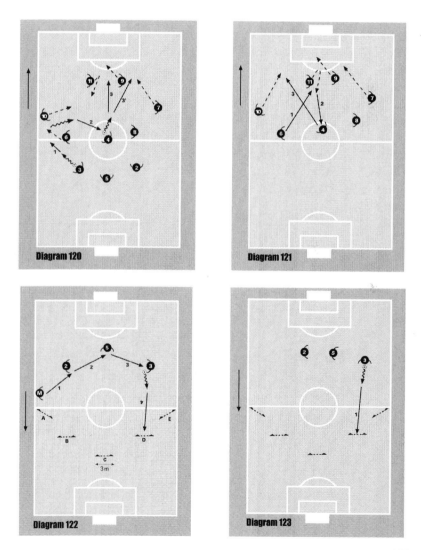

Diagram 120

Diagram 121

Diagram 122

Diagram 123

6.8 3:4:3 Exercises to improve the technical aspect of 3:4:3 (diagram 122)

Defenders 2, 5 and 3, having only 2 passes available, change the direction of play to allow for lateral support (posts A and B) or vertical support (E, D and C).

In fact during the match the opponents - depending on how they can organize their defensive stage - they can allow us to give lateral support or vertical support.
If the two options to play the ball are not available, then we only can kick the ball up-field.
The coach has to check the position of the body (meaning the visual line and position on the field) as the players receive the ball. He has to correct the technique and control the follow-through of the other defenders **(diagram 123 and 124)**.
Little by little, the players can come in and take their position till they complete the team with chains of players **(diagram 125 and 126)**.
With these exercises you can train the technique in each situation speeding up the execution .
If you practice it a bit slower, it can be a very useful exercise to warm up with the ball.

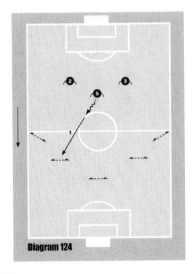

Diagram 124

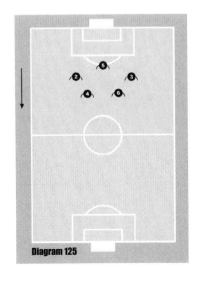

Diagram 125

108

6.9 Hand pass of the goalkeeper (diagram 127)

The goalkeeper passes the ball to 5 who then passes to 2. 2 vertically passes to 10. 10 moves inside and aims to 9, creating the space for the insertion of 7. The central forward 9, after receiving the ball (with a feint) opens up so that 7 can cross. In **diagram 128**, on the other hand, you can see the spaces taken by 9, 11 and 10 who are offering three points of reference: the near and far posts and the penalty spot; note the preventive covers of the midfield players 4, 6 and 8 for when the defenders play the

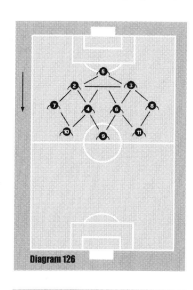

Diagram 126

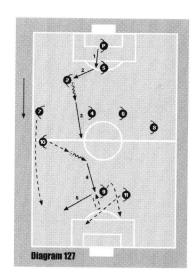

Diagram 127

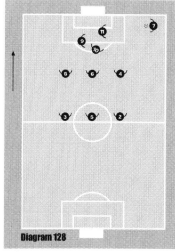

Diagram 128

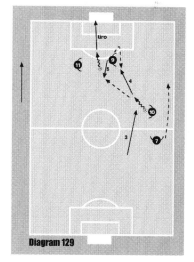

Diagram 129

ball back and the position of 2, 5 and 3.

Variable: the same movement, but with 9 not opening to 7 for the cross. 9 moves back to 10 who shoot at goal (diagram 129). In **diagram 130** we see the preventive covers of the teammates.

Variable 1: the same game, but with a different option, where 9 passes to 10, who is serving 11 to get into the area (**diagram 131**). In **diagram 132** we see the preventive covers of the other players.

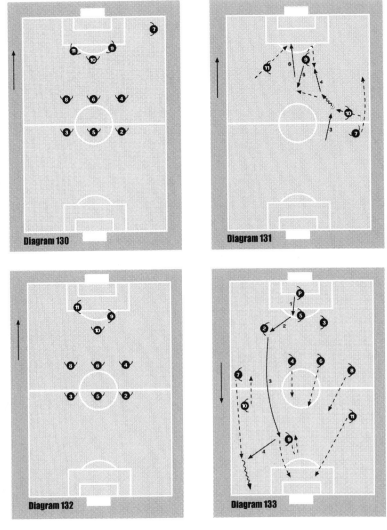

Diagram 130

Diagram 131

Diagram 132

Diagram 133

6.10 "Cable" movement (diagram 133)

This solution has such a name because 10 moves towards 2, freeing the space behind him. 2 passes to 9 (who feints). 9 controls or opens up to 7 for a cross. In **diagram 134** you can see the preventive covers.

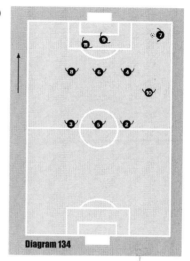

Diagram 134

We have already talked about the problem of position and team organization (in defense and attack). Now, we think, we should talk about the individual tactical basic principles. We have to say that the individual tactics completes the tactics related to the position and to the team, and vice versa. You cannot succeed if the players on the field don't have the pre-requisites we'll be speaking about. In other words, it would be like a house without a foundation.

Let's take a look at the basic principle of individual defense, meaning individual 1 v 1 position.

7.1 1 v 1 with one opponent and the ball in front or on the side

The defender is leaning forward, weight on the balls of the feet and the eyes on the ball. (This because the smaller you are the faster you can move around).

When we are facing a central attack, we need to protect the goal with the body. When the attack is lateral and you want to send the opponent to the outside, the feet should not be in line with the trajectory of the ball.

The tackle should be done when:

▶   the opponent in possession takes the foot off the ball.

With:

▶   the outer foot, if the opponent tries to move over on the outside;
▶   the inner foot, if the opponent tries to move over on the inside.

The tackle should be done by getting closer to the ball, with the weight-bearing foot almost parallel to the ball. If the weight is back too much, you can't hit the ball hard enough and you can easily lose the tackle.

It is important that the defender stays active, with feints he can force the opponent to make mistakes. It's fundamental not to let the ball get too close, especially if far from the goal, in wide spaces or with numerical inferiority; if the player in possession is close enough to shoot on goal, you should protect the goal with the body as much as possible.

If the attacker tries to force and win the 1 v 1 by sending the ball deep up field, the defender has two choices:

- if he did not let the ball get too close, he slides quickly on the ball (he's ahead of his opponent);
- if he let the ball get too close, he has to come in cutting off the opponent (he has no time to get on the ball); he must continue to act as a mobile shield and avoid obstruction.

7.2 1 v 1 with one opponent receiving the ball in front, with the defender attacking the opponent in front, on the right and on the left side

To what we have said before you must add that:
- it is necessary to be very fast as the ball is running, in other words you should try to get your opponent as far as possible from the goal;
- you have to choose the right moment to take your position, checking the distance;
- you should be able to run fast and to slow down, taking your position.

7.3 1 v 1 with the opponent receiving the ball and turning his back

- see the ball;
- be on the inside between the opponent and the goal;
- with a slow ball or a still opponent, you should try to contain from the inside;
- if the contain is not possible, check the opponent with one hand and never allow him to lean on you;
- do no allow the opponent to turn around;
- if he turns around, you should tackle him; you should do it when the player in possession is turned around half way, because that is the moment he is covering the ball least;
- if the player is very close the goal, you should stay on his side with arms open in order to block him.

7.4 1 v 1 with the ball far away

- see the ball and the opponent;
- stay on the inner side of the opponent and the goal;
- do not let the ball attack you;

The distance from the opponent varies:

▶ depending on the distance from the ball of both players;
▶ depending on where the action is taking place.

Let's look at the player in possession; generally speaking we can say that:

The marking is tight when near the ball, when the opponent is near the ball, when the opponent in possession can't see the goal or he sees it but can't play deep in the field. The marking is loose in all opposite cases.

7.5 A few training exercises

▶ Exercise A **(diagram 135)** ; A and B challenge each other with the ball not moving, alternating the right foot with the left foot.

▶ Exercise B **(diagram 136)**; A dribbles toward B who moves back changing his position depending on whether A is going right or left. *Variable:* Repeat the exercise turned to the right and to the left **(diagram 137)** and with the player in possession sending the ball deep toward the inside **(diagram 137b)**.

▶ Exercise C **(diagram 138)**; A tries a 1 v 1 and B neutralizes it since he did not allow the ball to get close. *Variable:* B has allowed the ball to get close **(diagram 139)**.

▶ Exercise D **(diagram 140)**; A passes to B (not moving) and C contains him moving to the inside and giving the ball back to A.

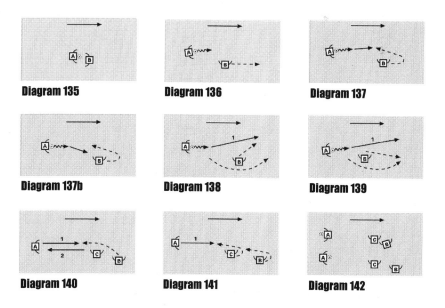

Diagram 135   **Diagram 136**   **Diagram 137**

Diagram 137b   **Diagram 138**   **Diagram 139**

Diagram 140   **Diagram 141**   **Diagram 142**

Repeat turning to the right and to the left. Variable: B moves forward and receives, C closes down and - when B tries to turn around - chooses the time for the tackle (**diagram 141**).

▶ Exercise E (**diagram 142**); the player in possession A places himself (with his body or head) so that he can or cannot see the attacker B and the defender C (who's marking him from the inside). C modifies his marking according to the visual behavior of A. Repeat the exercise turned to the right and to the left.

▶ Exercise F (**diagram 143**) ; central 1 v 1 with counterattack: when the attacker moves on with the ball, the defender starts defending. The attacker must come out from the opposite side and shoot or take on the goalkeeper 1 v 1. The defender, if in possession, has to counterattack on the starting line of the attacker. The defender can come out only with a 1 v 1 of the attacker. *Variable 1:* the attacker can receive a pass and attack; the defender can also come from right or left. *Variable 2:* lateral 1 v 1 with counterattack (**diagram 144**): the attacker can come out from either side. The defender can start in the same way as the attacker. *Variable 3:* (**diagram 145**); high lateral 1 v 1. *Variable 4:* repeat all the exercises with the receiver turning his back to the goal.

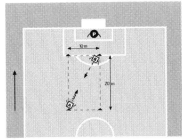

Diagram 143

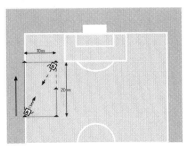

Diagram 144

Model Game
This is a game with set pairs plus the two goalkeepers; each player can challenge his direct opponent and visa versa; each team has a free player (staying in his half of the field only and who cannot be attacked when in possession) who is the only one able to challenge the unmarked opponent. This model game has several purposes:

▶   not being left out of the 1 v 1 situation; the free player is the only

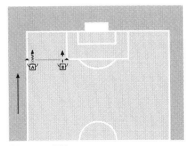

Diagram 145

116

one who can solve the situation;

- on-going training and practice of the different forms of 1 v 1 (lateral, from behind, in front, etc.);
- need of "reading" the marking during the defensive stage in a correct way;
- when moving towards the ball, getting used to going back to mark the opponent.

7.6 Attack basic principles

Let's focus now on the individual basic principles of the attack. There are two main elements:
- the action to elude the marking;
- the different ways of passing.

As for the action to elude the marking there are some aspects to remember:
- to elude the marking with no direction;
- to elude the marking with direction related to the situation of the player in possession;
- to elude the marking with direction related to your own marking duty;
- to elude the marking with direction related to both aspects;
- to elude the marking with direction.

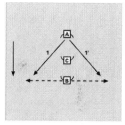

7.7 To elude the marking with no direction (diagram 146)

Diagram 146

This is when the player not in possession takes position in the gap between himself and his teammate in possession, avoiding the action of the defender. We want to remind you that for the action to elude the marking to have a sense, it has to be done by the player in the visual field of the leader.

7.8 To elude the marking with direction related to the situation of the player in possession (diagrams 147, 148, 149)

To elude the marking we not only have the "gap issue", but we also have a "space issue" on the 360°. The player moving to receive the ball will try to always be in a position that allows him to see the player in posses-

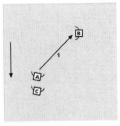
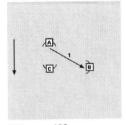
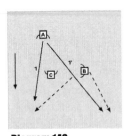

Diagram 147   **Diagram 148**   **Diagram 149**

sion and the opposing goal. Having stated that we should never unmark in line with the player in possession because the opponents' interception would cut off two of our players, there are three kinds of supports:

▶   backup;
▶   clearance;
▶   high support.

Backup: takes place behind the player in possession, when it's not possible to see the opponents' goal and, pressed from behind, it's possible to play only in the back. Do not do this too close to the player in possession, the defender could be able to come in also as passing back.

Clearance: a penetrating movement when the player in possession can see the goal but there is a defender keeping him from playing deep in the field.

High support: a movement deep up field to be done when the player in possession can see the goal and can play vertically.

7.9 To elude the marking related to your own marking duty (diagrams 150, 151, 152, 153)

There are four different positions (we pretend the player in possession can play vertically):

▶   long movement and penetration;
▶   penetrating and then long movement;
▶   In-depth disposition movement and narrowing;
▶   narrow movement and In-depth disposition.

In the first case there is a feint to play long (always done when the player in possession cannot see) that is in preparation of the second penetrating movement. Why do you have to play a feint? Two reasons:

▶   to fool the opponent;
▶   if done at the right time and in the right way, it should allow you to receive the ball.

118

The backward-upward movement has to be done when the opponent is marking loosely and from the inside. In other words he is strong in playing deep but weak in penetration.

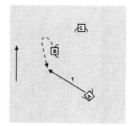

Diagram 150

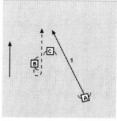

Diagram 151

On the other hand, the upward-backward feint (behind the defender) has to be realized when he's marking from the inside and with contact. The wide-inner movement will be done when the defender is marking with contact but from behind, leaving a lot

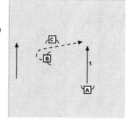

Diagram 152

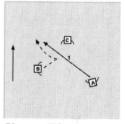

Diagram 153

of space inside. Of course we choose the narrowing movement (as a semicircle) when the defender stops the reception of the ball on the inside.

7.10 To elude the marking with direction related to the situation of the player in possession and to your own marking duty

It's not possible to precisely analyze the situation as above. We can say this situation is a 2 v 2 with infinite variables and it has to be solved applying the principles expressed above and the ones we will explain here.

7.11 Different kinds of passes

These are passes followed by a movement without the ball. It's clear that if these passes are addressed to players far away, their realization will be up to the players closer to the receiver.

Pass and go (diagrams 154, 155, 156, 157)
These passes are done in case the receiver is able to play the ball again, without any opposition.
We should consider:

▶ 1 - 2 or triangle (also vertical), to beat the opponent;

▶ pass and overlap, run behind the receiver who tends to create a 2 v 1;

▶ pass and cut in, trying to attack the blind side of the defender;

▶ pass and change, moving far away from the defender.

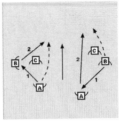

Diagram 154

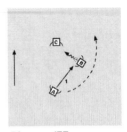

Diagram 155

*Pass and follow (**diagram 158**)*

During the pass the receiver cannot play the ball deep because he's closed down

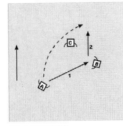

Diagram 156

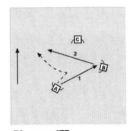

Diagram 157

by the defender. The player will keep supporting behind him.

1 - 2 - 3 *(diagram 159, 160)*

A player can pass and move on the marked teammate as long as there is a third player to give support. The receiver is supported by the third player and allows him to serve the deep movement of the player passing the ball.

This player has to stay behind the receiver until the supporter does not see him and is able to pass. Then he speeds up and moves deep up field. This is to avoid, in case of attack, the supporter finding himself in the situation of not having players covering him during the defensive stage. In the two diagrams we see two kinds of 1-2-3; this name comes from the

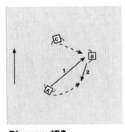

Diagram 158

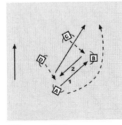

Diagram 159

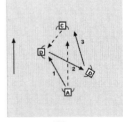

Diagram 160

120

number of passes necessary to obtain the combination; the same is true for the 1-2.

7.12 A few training exercises

We can use all the different situations of 2 v 1, 2 v 2, 3 v 3 with or without a set model game; as for the model games we can look at the match with set pairs - in the sphere of eluding the marking and regular matches - with or without free players. We can also look at the several methods of ball possession, with or without set goals.

8.1 Space training

Before talking about the formations, we have to train the players to move in space. Let me explain better. Very often you can see that:
▶ the players are all grouped near the ball;
▶ where there is no space it's impossible to play, meaning we never "switch the play".
This is the effect, but what is the cause? The cause is that the kids do not correctly perceive the space. What can we do?
The bibliography is full of solutions for this problem. We only say that the main elements you should consider to solve this issue are:
▶ a correct posture;
▶ the knowledge of the playing area and of the horizontal signs;
▶ consideration of other elements of the game, such as the team mates, the opponents, the ball.
Only when the player is in control of notions such as forward-back, left-right, high-low, inside-outside, etc. can we organize a geometrical phase of the formation with good chances of succeeding!

8.2 Organization of the matches

As for the way the junior matches are organized here in Italy, they don't help a gradual development of the youth and they don't respect the biological stages. We persist in holding 11 v 11 games with 10-11 year old children playing in facilities for 30 year old people. It would be like having kids playing volleyball with a net 8 ft. high or playing basketball on a regular court with a regular basket. The 7 v 7 of the colts (8-10 year olds) is considered an improvement, but it's not since it's still too complicated for kids so young. In fact:
▶ there are too many elements to keep in mind: 6 teammates, 7 opponents, the ball, the field;
▶ too many variables force the child to very complex analyses and he can't solve the micro-situations placed before him;

- only the more skilled children will be able to play, they will control the possession of the ball and they will allow the other kids to play only when strictly necessary.

I think we should organize games starting from 2 v 2 or 3 v 3 situations and then gradually increase the number of players. This would allow the child to consolidate what he has learned, gradually getting in contact with the increase of the variables and with the 11 v 11 situation of the adults. But with the system we use it's like building a house starting from the windows.

8.3 Choosing the formation

Let's begin from this concept: the role of the coach, especially with the youth, is to simplify the issues, not make them more complicated. I think the easiest formation is a 4:3:3 by zone. For several reasons:
- it's easier to identify the roles (wings, midfield players, backs, forwards, etc.)
- game chains;
- natural in-depth disposition of the formation width-wise and depth-wise;
- other formation's differences such as 4:4:2 where the forwards and the midfield players move by pairs; all this makes things more difficult.

Zone defense should be chosen because:
- the zone is a means, not an end, to better the collaboration among the players. In fact the zone requires mutual assistance and the participation of the whole group in the defensive stage. Some may not agree, but we want to remind you that:
- there are several systems to teach something and with active education we can have incredible response; but the effort has to come from the coach and not from the kids.

When we play in the backyard the children don't play man marking; Sven Goran Eriksson once said that the sliding toward the ball in a system by zone "is only the rationalization of what the kids do in the backyard games".

Of course as players grow, we can look for something different on the tactical level, but we should keep in mind that, if we did not build the player individually on a tactical-technical-human level at the beginning, we can't expect to successfully take him to the next level.

8.4 Formations for the very young players

I often hear the coaches talking about the colts (they play 7 v 7) and discussing if it's better to make them play with a formation or not.
Considering what I said about space training, here are a few proposals:

▸ some people play with a 3:2:1, others with 3:1:2 or 2:3:1 and more.

Keeping in mind the principle of simplicity, I propose a 3:3 for the following reasons:

▸ this formation has only two positions, whereas a soccer team has three positions: defense, midfield and attack. With a 3:3 (missing one line) there is a better possibility to exchange between defenders and attackers, so that everybody can have the thrill of scoring a goal or defending. The purpose is to have all the kids participating in the different game phases without bonding them to a specific role at such a young age!

Also available from Reedswain:

Also available from Reedswain:

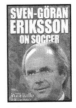

67716678R00077

Made in the USA
Middletown, DE
24 March 2018